Excel 2003

FOR

DUMMIES®

QUICK REFERENCE

by John Walkenbach and Colin Banfield

WILEY

Wiley Publishing, Inc.

Excel 2003 For Dummies® Quick Reference

Published by
Wiley Publishing, Inc.
111 River Street
Hoboken, NJ 07030

www.wiley.com

For general information on our other products and services or to obtain technical support, please contact our Customer Care Department within the U.S. at 800-762-2974, outside the U.S. at 317-572-3993, or fax 317-572-4002.

Wiley also publishes its books in a variety of electronic formats. Some content that appears in print may not be available in electronic books.

Library of Congress Control Number: 2003105670

ISBN: 0-7645-3987-6

Manufactured in the United States of America

10 9 8 7 6 5 4

1O/SS/QZ/QT/IN

About the Authors

John Walkenbach is a leading authority on spreadsheet software, and is principal of JWalk and Associates, Inc., a small, San Diego–based consulting firm that specializes in spreadsheet application development. John is the author of more than two dozen spreadsheet books and has written more than 300 articles and reviews for a variety of publications, including *PC World*, *InfoWorld*, *Windows* magazine, and *PC/Computing*. He also maintains The Spreadsheet Page, a popular Internet Web site (www.j-walk.com/ss), and is the developer of Power Utility Pak, an award-winning add-in for Microsoft Excel. John graduated from the University of Missouri and earned a master's and a Ph.D. from the University of Montana.

Colin Banfield has been working in the telecommunications field for over 22 years. Colin has been using spreadsheet programs for over 20 years and has used every major spreadsheet program at one time or another, including every version of Microsoft Excel for the PC. He works closely with acclaimed spreadsheet author and guru John Walkenbach in beta testing and providing valuable input for John's award-winning Power Utility Pak Excel add-in, as well as in reviewing many of John's spreadsheet books. Colin's largest Excel project to date is a comprehensive tool designed for telephone central office equipment configuration, pricing, and manufacturing, that is used by sales, engineering, and manufacturing personnel.

In his spare time, Colin writes and reviews books for Wiley Publishing, Inc., and enjoys photography, astronomy, chess, and expanding his musical repertoire.

Colin holds a BSc (Honors) in Electrical Engineering from the University of the West Indies.

Publisher's Acknowledgments

We're proud of this book; please send us your comments through our online registration form located at www.dummies.com/register/.

Some of the people who helped bring this book to market include the following:

Acquisitions, Editorial, and Media Development

Project Editor: Christine Berman
(Previous Edition: James Russell)

Acquisitions Editor: Tiffany Franklin

Copy Editor: John Edwards

Technical Editor: Kerwin McKenzie

Editorial Manager: Leah Cameron

Media Development Manager: Laura VanWinkle

Media Development Supervisor: Richard Graves

Editorial Assistant: Amanda Foxworth

Production

Project Coordinator: Ryan Steffen

Layout and Graphics: Joyce Haughey, Jacque Schneider, Julie Trippetti

Proofreaders: Laura Albert, Carl William Pierce, TECHBOOKS Production Services

Indexer: TECHBOOKS Production Services

Publishing and Editorial for Technology Dummies

Richard Swadley, Vice President and Executive Group Publisher

Andy Cummings, Vice President and Publisher

Mary C. Corder, Editorial Director

Publishing for Consumer Dummies

Diane Graves Steele, Vice President and Publisher

Joyce Pepple, Acquisitions Director

Composition Services

Gerry Fahey, Vice President of Production Services

Debbie Stailey, Director of Composition Services

Contents at a Glance

Table of Contents

Part XI: Working with Lists and External Data 155

Part XII: Goal Seeking and What-If Analysis 171

Part XIII: Analyzing Data with PivotTables 179

Microsoft Office Excel 2003

Spreadsheet software is a class of highly interactive computer programs with interfaces that consist of rows and columns that are displayed on-screen in a scrollable window. With Microsoft's popular Excel 2003 spreadsheet program, you can manipulate and analyze data in ways that would be impossible, very cumbersome, and definitely error prone for you to do manually. This part gives you the basics you need to get up and running quickly in Excel.

In this part . . .

- ✔ What You See
- ✔ Toolbar Table
- ✔ The Basics
- ✔ What You Can Do

What You See: The Excel Window

The following figure shows a typical Excel screen and points out some of the important parts. This terminology rears its ugly head throughout this book, so pay attention!

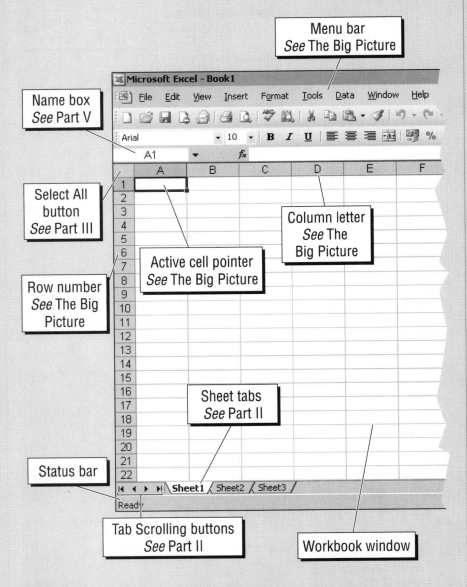

Menu bar
See The Big Picture

Name box
See Part V

Select All button
See Part III

Row number
See The Big Picture

Column letter
See The Big Picture

Active cell pointer
See The Big Picture

Sheet tabs
See Part II

Status bar

Tab Scrolling buttons
See Part II

Workbook window

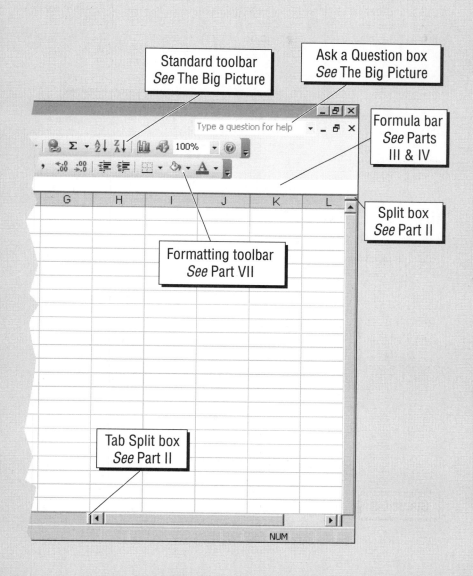

Standard toolbar
See The Big Picture

Ask a Question box
See The Big Picture

Formula bar
See Parts III & IV

Split box
See Part II

Formatting toolbar
See Part VII

Tab Split box
See Part II

Type a question for help

What You See: Dialog Boxes

Excel, like virtually every other Windows application, is big on dialog boxes. A *dialog box* is a small window that pops up in response to most of the commands that you issue. This window displays right on top of what you're doing — a sure sign that you must make some type of response to the dialog box before you can do anything else. The following figure shows a typical Excel dialog box.

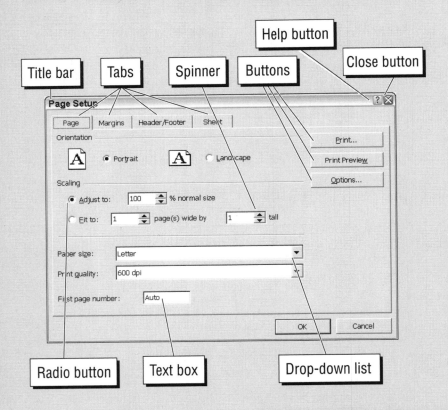

TIP 🎯 Notice that the various parts of a dialog box display text with a single underlined letter. You can use the Alt key along with this letter to jump to that particular component.

The following list describes the various types of controls and other parts that you meet up with as you discover the world of dialog boxes:

✔ **Button:** Clicking a dialog box button does something else (and the "something" depends on the button). If the text on the button ends in three dots (ellipsis points), clicking the text opens another dialog box.

✔ **Cancel button:** Click this button if you change your mind. None of the changes that you made to the dialog box take effect.

✔ **Check box (not shown):** A square box that you can click to turn the option on or off.

✔ **Drop-down list:** A list of things that you can choose from. These lists display a small downward-pointing arrow. Click the arrow to drop the list down and reveal more options.

✔ **Help button:** Click here and then click a dialog box control to find out what the control does. Excel displays a pop-up box that describes the control.

✔ **List box (not shown):** This box contains several items to choose from and usually displays a vertical scroll bar on the right that you can click to show more items in the list.

✔ **OK button:** Click this button after you make your dialog box selections and want to use those selections.

✔ **Radio (option) buttons:** Round buttons, usually appearing within a group box. Only one option button can be "on" at a time. After you click a radio button, the others in the group turn off.

✔ **Range selector (not shown):** A box that holds a cell or range address. You can click the button to select a range by pointing to it. (The dialog box shrinks to get out of your way.)

✔ **Spinner:** A control with two arrows (one pointing up, the other pointing down) that appears in conjunction with a text box. Clicking an arrow increases or decreases the number in the text box, depending on which arrow you click.

✔ **Tab:** Clicking a tab changes the dialog box to display a whole new set of controls. Not all dialog boxes use these tabs.

✔ **Text:** Words that explain what to do. You can click dialog box text, but nothing happens.

✔ **Text box:** A box in which you enter something — a number or text.

✔ **Title bar:** The colored bar at the top of the dialog box. Click and drag this bar to move the dialog box to a different part of the screen if the box is covering up something that you want to see.

Toolbar Table

One of the greatest timesaving features in Excel is its *toolbars*. By default, Excel displays the Standard and Formatting toolbars. The Standard toolbar contains buttons for such common tasks as opening and saving files, cutting and pasting data, and printing. Depending on the task that you're performing, Excel may automatically display additional toolbars on-screen.

Toolbars can float anywhere on-screen, or you can *dock* (attach) them on any side of the screen (left, right, top, or bottom). To move a floating toolbar, click the toolbar's title bar and drag it with the mouse. To detach a docked toolbar, click the dotted bar that precedes the first button on the toolbar and drag it with the mouse.

 TIP If you're unsure of the function of a particular toolbar button, you can hover the mouse cursor over the button to display a short description of the button's purpose.

To display additional toolbars, choose View➪Toolbars and select the appropriate toolbar from the list of names that appears.

The following table describes the buttons that you find on the Standard toolbar.

Tool/Button	Tool Name	What You Can Do	Shortcut	See
	New	Create an empty workbook file	Ctrl+N	The Big Picture
	Open	Open an existing file	Ctrl+O	The Big Picture
	Save	Save a workbook	Ctrl+S	The Big Picture
	Permission	Displays the Permission dialog box	n/a	——
	E-mail	E-mail worksheet data	n/a	Part II
	Print	Print a worksheet(s)	Ctrl+P	Part IX
	Print Preview	Display a preview of the print selection	n/a	Part IX
	Spelling	Initiate spell checking	F7	Part VI

Tool/Button	Tool Name	What You Can Do	Shortcut	See
	Research	Displays the Research task pane	Alt+Left Click	——
	Cut	Cut selected range to the Office Clipboard	Ctrl+X	Part III
	Copy	Copy selected range to the Office Clipboard	Ctrl+C	Part III
	Paste	Paste the contents of the Office Clipboard in the same or different document	Ctrl+V	Part III
	Format Painter	Copy the format of a cell or range to another cell or range	n/a	Part VII
	Undo	Undo up to the last 16 operations	Ctrl+Z	Part III
	Redo	Redo up to the last 16 operations	n/a	Part III
	Insert Hyperlink	Insert a hyperlink to another document or Web page	Ctrl+K	——
	AutoSum	Sum or perform other operations on a range of numbers	n/a	Part IV
	Sort Ascending	Sort a range in ascending order	n/a	Part XII
	Sort Descending	Sort a range in descending order	n/a	Part XII
	Chart Wizard	Create a chart	n/a	Part X
	Drawing	Display the drawing toolbar	n/a	——
100%	Zoom	Change the zoom factor of the active worksheet	n/a	Part II
	Microsoft Excel Help	Display the Office Assistant Help or the Help window	F1	The Big Picture

The Basics: Starting Excel

From the Windows XP Desktop, choose Start⇨All Programs⇨Microsoft Office⇨ Microsoft Office Excel 2003. If you're running an older version of Windows, choose Start⇨Programs⇨Microsoft Office⇨Microsoft Office Excel 2003.

The Excel screen appears. By default, Excel opens a blank workbook named Book1. You can change Excel's default startup workbook in several ways.

The Basics: Getting Acquainted with Excel

Excel files are known as *workbooks*. A single workbook can store as many sheets as can fit into memory, and these sheets stack like the pages in a note-book. Sheets are either worksheets (a normal spreadsheet-type sheet) or chart sheets (a special sheet that holds a single chart).

Most of the time, you work with worksheets — each of which contains exactly 65,536 rows and 256 columns. Rows number from 1 to 65,536, and columns use labels of letters. Column 1 is A, column 26 is Z, column 27 is AA, column 52 is AZ, column 53 is BA, and so on, up to column 256 (which is IV — not Roman numeral 4!).

The intersection of a row and a column is known as a *cell*. A quick calculation with Excel tells me that 65,536 rows x 256 columns works out to 16,777,216 cells — which should be enough for most people. Cells have addresses, which Excel bases on the row and column that the cells are in. The upper-left cell in a worksheet is A1, and the cell way down at the bottom is IV65536. Cell K9 (also known as the dog cell) is the intersection of the 11th column and the ninth row. A cell in Excel can hold a number, some text, a formula, or nothing at all.

In Excel, one of the cells in a worksheet is always the *active cell*. The active cell is the one that's selected, and it appears with a thicker border. The active cell's row number and column letter are also shaded. The cell's contents appear in the *Formula Bar*. (***See also*** "What You See: The Excel Window," earlier in this part, for details about the Formula Bar.)

Navigating with the keyboard

With more than 16 million cells in a worksheet, you need ways to move to specific cells. Fortunately, Excel provides you with many techniques to move around a worksheet. As always, you can use either your mouse or the keyboard on your navigational journeys. The following table lists the keystrokes that enable you to move through a worksheet.

Keys	Action
Up arrow	Moves the active cell up one row
Down arrow	Moves the active cell down one row
Left arrow	Moves the active cell one column to the left
Right arrow	Moves the active cell one column to the right
PgUp	Moves the active cell up one screen
PgDn	Moves the active cell down one screen
Alt+PgDn	Moves the active cell right one screen
Alt+PgUp	Moves the active cell left one screen
Ctrl+Backspace	Scrolls to display the active cell
Up arrow*	Scrolls the screen up one row (active cell doesn't change)
Down arrow*	Scrolls the screen down one row (active cell doesn't change)
Left arrow*	Scrolls the screen left one column (active cell doesn't change)
Right arrow*	Scrolls the screen right one column (active cell doesn't change)

* With Scroll Lock on

Navigating with the mouse

Navigating through a worksheet with a mouse works just as you'd expect. Just click a cell, and it becomes the active cell. If the cell that you want to activate isn't visible in the workbook window, you can use the scroll bars to scroll the window in any direction, as follows:

- To scroll one cell, click one of the arrows on the scroll bar.

- To scroll by a complete screen, click either side of the scroll bar's slider button (the large center button).

- To scroll faster, drag the slider.

- To scroll a long distance vertically, press and hold Shift while dragging the slider button.

Notice that only the active workbook window displays scroll bars. If you activate a different window, its scroll bars appear.

Understanding the Excel menu bar

In Excel, the menu bar is actually a toolbar. As such, you can move it around on-screen by dragging it (*See also* "Toolbar Table," in this part). The only difference between the menu bar and any other toolbar is that the menu bar contains a list of menus instead of buttons.

For each menu on the Excel menu bar, you have both a "short" and a "full" list of menu items. When you click a menu, Excel displays the short menu list by default. The short menu list shows only the commands that you most commonly use. Clicking the small arrow at the bottom of the short menu list reveals the full menu list. (Clicking a menu on the menu bar while holding down the mouse button for a few seconds also reveals the full menu list.) After you click one of the normally hidden commands, it receives a "promotion" and appears thereafter among the commands in the short menu list.

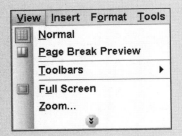

 If you find the short and full menus confusing, you can turn the short menu option off by choosing View⇨Toolbars⇨Customize. Select the Options tab in the Customize dialog box that appears, and choose the Always Show Full Menus check box. (This setting applies to all Office applications, so if you set it in Excel, you automatically set it in Word, PowerPoint, and so on.)

The Basics: Getting Help

Excel provides several methods for the user to get help easily, as the following list describes:

- **Ask a Question box:** Type a question in plain English in the *Help box* at the far right of the menu bar. After you press Enter, a list of related help topics appears. Click the appropriate topic to access the Help window for that topic.

- **Dialog box help:** If a dialog box is on-screen, click the Help button in the title bar (if it displays a question mark). Excel displays a help window that provides a description of the options in the dialog box. *See also* "What You See: Dialog Boxes," earlier in this part.

- **Office Assistant:** The animated Office Assistant monitors your actions while you work. If a more efficient way of performing an operation exists, the Assistant can tell you about it.

  If the Office Assistant isn't visible, select Help⇨Show the Office Assistant in the Standard toolbar. You can drag the assistant to any location on-screen.

- **"What's This?" help:** Press Shift+F1, and the mouse pointer turns into a question mark. You can then click virtually any part of the screen to get a description of the object.

The Office Assistant takes the form of an animated character that floats over the Excel screen. You can choose among eight different characters. To change the character, right-click the Assistant and select Choose Assistant from the shortcut menu that appears. In the Gallery tab of the Office Assistant dialog box that appears, click the Back or Next button to display the available characters. Click OK to select the new character.

The Office Assistant provides the following types of help:

- It displays a Tip of the Day whenever you start Excel (you can turn this feature on and off by right-clicking the Assistant, selecting Options from the shortcut menu, and checking or unchecking the Show the Tip of the Day at startup check box).

- It watches you work and tells you if a more efficient way to perform an operation exists. A yellow light bulb appears next to the Assistant (or on the Microsoft Excel Help button) if the Assistant has a tip for you. Click the light bulb to read the tip.

- ✔ It provides automatic help with certain tasks. If you're about to create a chart, for example, the Assistant asks whether you need help.

- ✔ It responds to natural language questions. Just type your question in the Assistant's box and click Search (that underline you see under the S in Search indicates a *hotkey combination*, which means you can press Alt+S to accomplish the same thing as clicking the button).

TIP ✔ If you find that the Office Assistant is sometimes too helpful and it gets distracting, customize it to your liking: Right-click the Assistant, and choose Options from the shortcut menu. The Office Assistant dialog box appears with the Options tab selected.

TIP ✔ A feature in the Options tab of the Office Assistant dialog box enables you to turn the Assistant on and off. To turn the Assistant off, deselect the check box next to the Use the Office Assistant label. To turn the Assistant on, choose Help⇨Show the Office Assistant from the menu bar.

Remember: You can choose Help⇨Hide the Office Assistant from the menu bar to hide the Assistant if it is on. Hiding the Assistant isn't the same as turning the Assistant off. Hiding the Assistant simply hides the icon from view. If you later click the Microsoft Excel Help button on the toolbar, the Assistant reappears. If you turn the Assistant off and then click the Microsoft Excel Help button, Excel displays the Help window but doesn't show the Assistant.

The Basics: Creating an Empty Workbook File

After you start Excel, it automatically creates a new (empty) workbook that it calls Book1. If you're starting a new project from scratch, you can use this blank workbook.

You can create another blank workbook in any of the following three ways:

- ✔ Click the New button on the Standard toolbar.
- ✔ Press Ctrl+N.
- ✔ Choose File⇨New and click Blank Workbook in the New Workbook task pane.

Any of these methods creates a blank default workbook.

The Basics: Saving a Workbook File

If you save a workbook, Excel saves the copy in memory to your disk — overwriting the previous copy of the file. If you save a workbook for the first time, Excel displays its Save As dialog box.

To save the active workbook to disk, choose File⇨Save. Or you can also use any of the following methods to save a file:

- ✔ Click the Save button on the Standard toolbar.
- ✔ Press Ctrl+S.
- ✔ Press Shift+F12.

If you haven't saved the file, Excel prompts you for a name by opening its Save As dialog box. **See also** "Saving a workbook under a different name," in Part I.

The Basics: Opening a Workbook File

Excel's primary file type is known as a *workbook file*. If you open a workbook in Excel, the entire file loads into memory, and any changes that you make occur only in the copy that's in memory.

To open an existing workbook file, follow these steps:

1. Choose File⇨Open from the menu bar to access the Open dialog box.

   You can also use any of the following methods to open the Open dialog box:

   - Click the Open button on the Standard toolbar.
   - Press Ctrl+O.
   - Press Ctrl+F12.

2. Specify the folder that contains the file in the Look in drop-down list.

3. Select the workbook file in the selected folder and click Open, or double-click the filename.

   > **TIP** You can select more than one file in the Open dialog box. The trick is to press and hold Ctrl while you click the filenames. After you select all the files that you want, click Open. (*See also* "Switching Among Open Workbooks," in Part I, for more information about opening and using multiple files.)

The following are other ways to open a workbook file:

- **Double-click the workbook name in any folder window.** If Excel isn't running, it starts automatically. Or, you can drag a workbook icon into the Excel window to load the workbook.

- **Choose it from the File menu.** At the bottom of the File menu, Excel provides a list of files you've worked with recently. If the file that you want appears in this list, you can choose it directly from the menu.

- **Open the file automatically.** If you find that you use the same workbook every time that you start Excel, you can make this workbook open automatically whenever Excel starts. Just move the workbook to the XLStart folder. In Windows 2000 or XP, the XLStart folder normally resides in C:\Documents and Settings\username\Application Data\Microsoft\Excel. In Windows 9x, the XLStart folder normally resides in C:\Program Files\Microsoft Office\Office10.

The Basics: Closing a Workbook File and Exiting Excel

If you're no longer working with a workbook file, you may want to close the file so that you can work on other files without distraction. Closing unneeded files also frees memory and minimizes potential screen clutter.

To close the unneeded file or files, follow these steps:

1. If you have multiple files open, first ensure that the file you want to close is active. Choose the Window menu command, and select the file from the list of names in the bottom part of the menu. This step is unnecessary if you only have one file open.

2. Use any of the following methods to close the file:

   - Select File⇨Close.

   - Click the Close button in the workbook's title bar (or on the menu bar if the workbook is maximized).

   - Double-click the Control button in the workbook's title bar (or on the menu bar if the workbook is maximized).

   - Press Ctrl+F4.

   - Press Ctrl+W.

   If you've made any changes to your workbook since the last time you saved it, Excel asks whether you want to save the changes before closing it.

    TIP To close all open workbooks, press Shift and choose File⇨Close All. (This command appears only if you hold down Shift while you click the File menu.) Excel closes each workbook, prompting you to save each unsaved workbook.

3. To exit Excel, choose File⇨Exit.

What You Can Do: Create and Analyze Data

N23		fx					
	A	B	C	D	E	F	
1							
2		Five Year Plan					
3		Key Financial Indicators ($000)					
4							
5		YEAR 1	YEAR 2	YEAR 3	YEAR 4	YEAR 5	
6	Revenue	5,774	12,680	24,550	44,895	72,163	
7	Gross margin - $	3,002	6,594	12,521	22,448	36,081	
8	Gross margin - %	52%	52%	51%	50%	50%	
9	Operating expenses	7,161	7,432	8,703	9,637	8,610	
10	Operating income	(4,159)	(839)	3,817	12,810	27,471	
11							
12	Return On Investment - Operating income	-72%	-7%	16%	29%	38%	
13							
14	Increase (decrease) in cash and ST invest.	(5,870)	(2,274)	2,634	10,728	24,543	
15	Cash and ST invest. - beginning of year	10,000	14,130	11,856	14,490	25,217	
16	Cash and ST invest. - end of year	4,130	11,856	14,490	25,217	49,760	
17							

key indicators / revenue / expenses / income statement / balance sh

Setting up data for analysis is a fundamental task in Excel. For example, you can create a simple spreadsheet to analyze the impact of different interest rates on a monthly loan payment or a more complex spreadsheet to analyze the monthly performance of salespeople serving different territories.

1. Get started by

Creating an Empty Workbook File, The Big Picture

Entering and Editing Worksheet Data, Part III

Saving a Workbook File, The Big Picture

2. Work on your project by

Creating and Using Names, Part V

Auditing Your Work, Part VI

Analyzing Your Work, Parts XII and XIII

3. Add finishing touches by

Formatting Your Data, Part VII

Printing Your Work, Part VIII

What You Can Do: Show Data Graphically

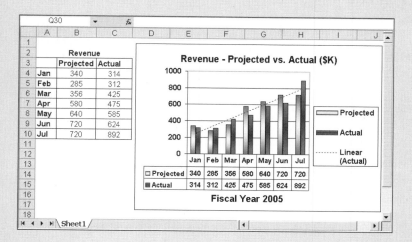

Displaying data in a well-conceived chart can make it more understandable, and you can often make your point more quickly.

1. Get started by

Opening a Workbook File, The Big Picture

Using the Chart Wizard, Part IX

2. Work on your project by

Adding Elements to Your Chart, Part IX

Adding a Legend to Your Chart, Part IX

Displaying a Data Table in Your Chart, Part IX

3. Add finishing touches by

Changing the Chart Type, Part IX

Modifying Chart Elements, Part IX

What You Can Do: Import Data for Analysis

	P12	▼		*f*ₓ	9951061000			
	A	B	C	M	N	O	P	
1	**Stock Quotes Provided by** N							
2	Click here to visit MSN Money							
3				**Market Cap**	**EPS**	**P/E Ratio**	**# Shares Out**	
4	Nortel Networks Limited	Chart	News	9,061,347,037	-0.93		3,839,554,000	
5	AT&T Corp.	Chart	News	13,250,639,788	-16.4		770,386,000	
6	Lucent Technologies Inc.	Chart	News	5,916,104,788	-3.47		3,607,381,000	
7	AOL Time Warner Inc.	Chart	News	45,805,201,478	-9.98		4,305,000,000	
8	CITIGROUP ADJ CM Q	Chart	News	0	0	0	0	
9	Pfizer Inc	Chart	News	180,551,400,499	1.53	19.5	6,162,164,000	
10	Citigroup Inc.	Chart	News	166,418,234,108	3.22	10.3	5,056,768,000	
11	Medtronic, Inc.	Chart	News	53,075,220,000	1.06	41.3	1,220,120,000	
12	General Electric Company	Chart	News	225,889,092,292	1.51	15.2	9,951,061,000	
13								
14					External Data ▼ ×			
15								
16								

Sheet1 \ **Sheet2** / Sheet3 /

Excel enables you to easily import data from various sources (a text file, the Web, or an external database) for analysis. Importing data can save you a lot of time that you would otherwise spend entering the data manually. After the data is imported, you can use Excel tools to analyze or otherwise utilize the data for your calculations.

1. Get started by

Creating an Empty Workbook File, The Big Picture

Importing Data from a Text File or the Web, Part XI

2. Work on your project by

Refreshing Imported Data, Part XI

Goal Seeking and What-If Analysis, Part XII

Analyzing Data with PivotTables, Part XIII

3. Add finishing touches by

Formatting Your Data, Part VII

Printing Your Work, Part VIII

Part I

Using Workbook Files

Working with files is critical to using any software. Microsoft Excel files are known as *workbooks*. This part covers the procedures that you need to know to manage workbook files efficiently.

In this part . . .

Changing the Default File Location

After you open a file in Excel, by default the Open dialog box points to the My Documents folder as the starting location to open files. If you keep frequently used documents in a different folder, you may want the Open dialog box to point to this different folder instead to save some navigation steps. To change this default folder, follow these steps:

1. Choose Tools⇨Options from the menu bar.

2. In the Options dialog box that appears, select the General tab.

3. In the Default File Location text box, enter the path of the new default starting location to open files. For example, if your new default file location is in a subfolder named Excel, which itself is in a folder named Program Files on drive C, enter the path **C:\Program Files\Excel**.

4. Click OK

Creating Multiple Windows (Views) for a Workbook

Sometimes, you may want to view two different parts of a worksheet at once. Or, you may want to see more than one sheet in the same workbook. You can accomplish either of these actions by displaying your workbook in one or more additional windows.

To create a new view of the active workbook, choose Window⇨New Window from the menu bar. Excel displays a new window for the active workbook. To help you keep track of the windows, Excel appends a colon and a number to each window.

Dep-budg.xls:1

	A	B	C	D	E	F
1		Quarter 1	Quarter 2	Quarter 3	Quarter 4	
2	Salaries	$375,000.00	$375,000.00	$375,000.00	$375,000.00	
3	Travel	$ 3,200.00	$ 3,200.00	$ 3,200.00	$ 3,200.00	
4	Supplies	$ 25,000.00	$ 25,000.00	$ 25,000.00	$ 25,000.00	
5	Facility	$ 13,500.00	$ 13,500			
6	Total	$416,700.00	$416,700			

Dep-budg.xls:2

	A	B	C	D
1		Quarter 1	Quarter 2	Quarter 3
2	Salaries	$490,000.00	$490,000.00	$490,000.00
3	Travel	$ 2,200.00	$ 2,200.00	$ 2,200.00
4	Supplies	$ 18,500.00	$ 18,500.00	$ 18,500.00
5	Facility	$ 22,900.00	$ 22,900.00	$ 22,900.00
6	Total	$533,600.00	$533,600.00	$533,600.00

Operations / Manufacturing

See also "Arranging Windows Automatically," in Part II to see all your workbook views simultaneously.

Remember: A single workbook can have as many views (that is, separate windows) as you want.

Displaying multiple windows for a workbook also makes copying information from one worksheet to another easier. You can use Excel's drag-and-drop procedures to copy a cell, a range, a graphic object, or a chart.

Deleting a Workbook File

If you no longer need a workbook file, you may want to delete it from your floppy disk or hard drive to free space and reduce the number of files that appear in the Open dialog box.

You can delete files by using standard Windows techniques (for example, by using the Delete option in Windows Explorer or in a third-party file manager program), or you can delete files directly from Excel by following these steps:

1. Choose either File➪Open or File➪Save As from the menu bar to open a dialog box that displays a list of filenames.

2. Right-click a filename, and choose Delete from the shortcut menu that appears. Depending on how your system is set up, you may need to confirm this action.

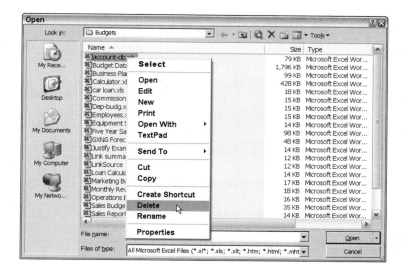

TIP

> If your system is set up to use the Recycle Bin, you can often recover a file that you delete accidentally. Before you empty the Recycle Bin, open it and drag out any items that you want to save.

Opening Nonstandard Files

In The Big Picture part, we describe the procedure for opening standard workbook files. In this section, we show you how to open non-Excel files, older Excel files, and workspace files.

Opening a non-Excel or older Excel file

Excel 2003 can open files that weren't saved in its native format by using filters to open the foreign file as a workbook file.

To open a non-Excel or older Excel file, follow these steps:

1. Choose File⇨Open to display the Open dialog box.

2. Select the file type from the Files of type drop-down list box.

3. Specify the folder that contains the file in the Look In drop-down list.

4. Select the file and click Open, or double-click the filename.

Excel can open files saved in any earlier version of Excel (*.XLS, *.XLT, *.XLC, *.XLW, *.XLM) or files saved in Lotus 1-2-3 (*.WKS, *.WK1, *.WK3, *.WK4), Quattro Pro (*.WQ1, *.WB1, *.WB3), text (*.CSV, *.TXT, *.PRN, *.DIF, *.SLK), Microsoft Works for DOS or V2.0 for Windows (*.WKS), HTML (*.HTM, *.MHT), XML (*.XML), Access databases (*.mdb, *.mde) and Dbase (*.dbf) files.

Opening a workspace file

To open a workspace file, follow the steps outlined for opening a non-Excel or older Excel file, except in Step 2, select Workspaces (*.XLW) in the Files of type drop-down list box. Excel opens all the workbooks that you originally saved in the workspace.

See also "Saving a workspace file," later in this part.

Protecting a Workbook File

Sometimes, you may want to protect a workbook by preventing users from adding or deleting sheets. Or, you may want to ensure that the workbook's window size or position doesn't change. To protect a workbook, follow these steps:

1. Choose Tools⇨Protection⇨Protect Workbook from the menu bar to open the Protect Workbook dialog box.

2. Select the appropriate check box, as follows:

   - *Structure* prevents any of the following changes to a workbook sheet: adding, deleting, moving, renaming, hiding, or unhiding.

   - *Windows* protects the workbook window from being moved or resized.

3. Supply a password in the Password (optional) text box if you feel that you need a level of protection.

4. Click OK.

To remove protection from a protected workbook, choose Tools⇨Protection⇨Unprotect Workbook and enter a password if you used one to protect the workbook.

Recovering Workbook Files after a System Crash

Excel 2003 enables you to recover previously opened files following a system crash, application lockup, or power failure. Excel analyzes the files that you were working on for errors. Depending on the extent of the error, Excel repairs or recovers information in the working files. Usually, but not in all cases, Excel can recover unsaved data.

The Document Recovery task pane displays all files that were rescued from the last Excel session and indicates whether the files were recovered by placing the word `Recovered` in brackets next to the filename. To open, delete, or save a recovered file, follow these steps:

1. Place the mouse cursor over the recovered file in the Document Recovery task pane.

   An arrow appears on the right side of the filename.

2. Click the arrow next to the recovered file.

   A menu appears.

3. Perform one of the following actions from the menu:

   - Select Open to view the file.

     You can also click the filename directly to open the file.

   - Select Save As to save the file.

     Save it by using the same or a new filename.

   - Select Delete to delete the file.

   - Select Show Repairs to view what repairs Excel made (if any).

4. Repeat Steps 1 and 2 for each recovered file.

You can also click the filename to open the file.

By default, Excel saves information for document recovery every 10 minutes. To change this default interval, follow these steps:

1. Choose Tools⇨Options from the menu bar, and click the Save tab in the Options dialog box that appears.

2. Make sure that the Save AutoRecover info every check box is selected, and enter the new recovery save interval in the Minutes text box.

   You can enter from 1 to 120 minutes in the Minutes text box.

3. Click OK.

You can turn the Document Recovery task pane on and off whenever Excel lists recovered files by choosing View⇨Toolbars⇨Document Recovery from the menu bar. This procedure is different from that of clicking the Close button in the Document Recovery task pane, which requires you to delete the recovered files unless you want to view them the next time that you start Excel.

You don't want to use the document recovery feature as a substitute for periodically saving files, because Excel can't always recover unsaved data. And the recovery feature can't help you if you close your files normally without saving changes.

Remember: If the word `Original` appears in brackets next to a file in the Document Recovery task pane, Excel hasn't recovered the file. The version of the file that you open with an `Original` designation is based on the last manual save.

Saving Files

In The Big Picture part, we describe the procedure for saving standard workbook files. In this section, we show you how to save a workbook file under a different name, save a workbook file in a different file format, save your work automatically, and save a workspace file.

Saving a workbook under a different name

Sometimes, you may want to keep multiple versions of your work by saving each successive version under a different name.

To save a workbook with a different name, follow these steps:

1. Choose File⇨Save As from the menu bar to open the Save As dialog box.

2. Select the folder in which you want to store the workbook from the Save In drop-down list.

3. Enter a new filename in the File Name text box. (You don't need to include the XLS file extension.)

4. Click Save.

Excel creates a new copy with a different name, but the original version of the file remains intact. (Notice that the original file is no longer open.)

You can also use the File⇨Save As command to make a backup copy of a workbook simply by saving the file (with the same name) to a floppy disk, a different drive, or a different folder. Excel remembers only the last place that it saves the file, however, so you may want to save the workbook again in its original location.

To prevent others from opening a workbook or from making changes to it, select Tools⇨General Options in the Save As dialog box and enter a password in the Save Options dialog box that appears.

Saving a workbook in a different or older file format

To share a file with someone who uses an application that opens files in a format that is different from Excel 2003, such as a much older version of Excel or a version Lotus 1-2-3, be sure to save the file in a format that the application can read.

To save a workbook in a different file format, follow these steps:

1. Choose File⇨Save As from the menu bar.

2. Select the format in which you want to save the file from the Save As Type drop-down list.

3. Click Save.

Remember: Excel 2003, Excel 2002, Excel 2000, and Excel 97 all use the same file format so that you can use the File⇨Save command (or click the Save toolbar button) if you're saving files to share with users of Excel 2002, Excel 2000, or Excel 97.

To save your workbook as a Web page so that people can view it within a browser, choose File⇨Save as Web Page from the menu bar. In the Save As dialog box that appears, select the Entire Workbook radio button (this is the default setting), give the file a name with the HTM extension, and click Save.

Excel can save to any earlier version of Excel workbook (*.XLS, *.XLW), Lotus 1-2-3 (*.WKS, *.WK1, *.WK3, *.WK4), Quattro Pro for DOS (*.WQ1), text (*.CSV, *.TXT, *.PRN, *.DIF, *.SLK), HTML (*.HTM, *MHT), XML (*.XML), and so on.

Saving a workspace file

The term *workspace* means all the workbooks and their screen positions and window sizes — sort of a snapshot of Excel's current state.

You may have a project that uses two or more workbooks, and you may also like to arrange the windows in a certain way to make them easy to access. Fortunately, Excel enables you to save your entire workspace to a file. Then you can open the workspace file, and Excel is set up exactly as it was when you saved your workspace. To save your workspace, follow these steps:

1. Choose File⇨Save Workspace from the menu bar.

2. Use the filename that Excel proposes (resume.xlw or resume), or enter a different name in the File Name text box.

The file extension appears only if you turn off the Hide file extensions for known file types option on the View tab of the Folder Options dialog box in Windows Explorer. This option is on by default.

3. Click the Save button, and Excel saves the workspace file to a disk.

A workspace file doesn't include the workbook files themselves — only the information that Excel needs to recreate the workspace. Excel saves the workbooks in standard workbook files. If you distribute a workspace file to a coworker, therefore, make sure that you also include the workbook files that the workspace file refers to.

Switching among Open Workbooks

If you have multiple workbooks open, the workbooks usually appear maximized on-screen so that you can view only one workbook at a time.

To switch the active display among workbooks, use either of the following methods:

- ✔ Click the Window item on the menu bar, and select one of the workbook names in the lower portion of the menu that appears.

- ✔ Press Ctrl+F6 or Ctrl+Tab to cycle the active display among the open workbooks.

Working with Workbook Templates

A *workbook template* is basically a workbook file that contains one or more worksheets that are set up with formatting and formulas and are ready for you to enter data and get immediate results. A workbook template can use any of Excel's features, such as charts, formulas, and macros. Excel includes templates that automate the common tasks of filling in invoices, expense statements, and purchase orders. You can also create your own templates.

Creating a workbook template

To save a workbook as a template, follow these steps:

1. Choose File➪Save As from the menu bar to open the Save As dialog box.

2. Select Template from the Save As Type drop-down list box.

   Excel displays the Templates folder in the Save In drop-down list box.

3. Select the Templates folder or a subfolder within the Templates folder, and save the template workbook in the folder that you choose.

   To create a new folder in the Templates folder in which you can save the template, click the Create New Folder button in the Save As dialog box and give the new folder a name.

4. Enter a name for the template in the File name box, and click Save.

Excel saves templates with an XLT file extension.

To prevent overwriting the template file when you create a new workbook from a template, always save your templates in the Templates folder or a subfolder within the Templates folder.

Creating a workbook from a template

If you create a new workbook that you base on a template, Excel creates a copy of the template in memory so that the original template remains intact. The default workbook name is the template name with a number appended. For example, if you create a new workbook based on a template by the name of Report.xlt, the workbook default name is Report1.xls. The first time that you save a workbook that you create from a template, Excel displays the Save As dialog box so that you can give the file a new name.

To create a workbook from a template, follow these steps:

1. Choose File⇨New from the menu bar.

   Excel displays the New Workbook task pane.

2. In the New Workbook task pane, select a link to the template you want to use from one the following categories:

   • In the Templates category, click the On my computer link to display the Templates dialog box. Templates that you create appear on the General tab if you save your template files in the Templates folder. If you save your files in a subfolder within the Templates folder, your files appear on the tab with the subfolder's name. Templates that Excel supplies appear on the Spreadsheet Solutions tab. You can double-click the filename in a tab to open a copy of the template.

   • In the Templates category, click the Templates home page link to open a browser window that displays the Microsoft Office Templates home page. This page provides several Office templates that it groups in various categories and subcategories. Click a category and subcategory heading until you find an Excel template that you want to use. On the page that contains the Excel template, click the Download Now button and follow the instructions to import a copy of the template into Excel.

   • In the Templates category, click the On my Web sites link to display the New from Templates on my Web Sites dialog box. In the File Name drop-down text box, type the URL (Web address) of the template location and click the Create

Now button to import a copy of the template into Excel. Notice that you must have an active Internet connection for this option to work.

You can click the arrow in the File Name drop-down text box to select the URL of previously used templates.

- Under the Recently used templates category, Excel 2003 displays the last four templates used. You can click one of these filenames to open a copy of the template directly.

3. Save the workbook after you enter the appropriate data in the template copy. *See also* "Saving Files," earlier in this part.

See also "Creating a workbook template," earlier in this part.

Creating a default workbook template

You can create a default workbook template that defines the formatting or content of the new (blank) workbooks that open after you start Excel. Excel bases blank workbooks that you create by clicking the New button on the standard toolbar (or by pressing Ctrl+N) on the default workbook template. The default workbook template that you create replaces Excel's built-in default workbook template.

Follow these steps to create a default workbook template:

1. Create a new workbook. *See also* "The Basics: Creating an Empty Workbook File," in The Big Picture.

2. Add or delete as many worksheets as you want to appear in new workbooks. ***See also*** "Adding a New Worksheet" and "Deleting a Worksheet," both in Part II.

3. Apply the desired formatting, sheet names, text, style, and so on. ***See also*** Part VII if you need help applying different formatting options.

4. Choose File⇨Save As from the menu bar, and select Template from the Save As Type drop-down list box.

5. Locate an xlstart folder in the Save In drop-down box.

   Excel can use more than one xlstart folder and will open all files located in these folders on startup. The locations of the xlstart folders depend on the version of Windows that is installed in your system.

   For Windows 2000 and XP, the xlstart folders reside in the `C:\Documents and Settings\`*Username*`\Application Data\Microsoft\Excel` and `C:\Program Files\ Microsoft Office\Office 11` folders, respectively. *Username* is your login username.

6. Type **book.xlt** in the File Name text box.

7. Click Save.

All new (blank) workbooks that you create are now replicas of the book.xlt workbook that you saved in Step 7.

You can always edit the book.xlt file or delete it if you no longer want to use it.

Although you can't change the locations of the xlstart folders, Excel allows you to place startup files (including book.xlt) in a folder of your choice. Choose Tools⇨Options to display the Options dialog box, and select the General tab. In the At startup, open all files in box, enter the complete path to your chosen folder. On startup, Excel then opens all files in your chosen folder in addition to any files that are in the xlstart folders.

Part II

Working with Worksheets

A workbook can consist of any number of *worksheets*. Each sheet has a tab that appears at the bottom of the workbook window. In this part, we discuss several useful things that you can do with worksheets.

In this part . . .

Activating Worksheets

To activate a different worksheet, just click its tab. If the tab for the sheet that you want to activate isn't visible, use the tab scrolling buttons to scroll the sheet tabs. You also can use the following shortcut keys to activate a different sheet:

- ✔ **Ctrl+PgUp:** Activates the previous sheet, if you have one.

- ✔ **Ctrl+PgDn:** Activates the next sheet, if you have one.

Adding a New Worksheet

You can add a new worksheet to a workbook in the following three ways:

- ✔ Choose Insert➪Worksheet from the menu bar.

- ✔ Right-click a sheet tab, choose Insert from the shortcut menu that appears, and select Worksheet from the General tab in the Insert dialog box.

- ✔ Press Shift+F11.

Excel inserts a new worksheet before the active worksheet; the new worksheet then becomes the active worksheet. The default name that Excel gives to the worksheet is the word Sheet, followed by a number — for example Sheet4, Sheet5, and so on.

Arranging Windows Automatically

If you want all your unhidden workbook windows visible on-screen, you can move and resize them manually — or you can have Excel do it automatically.

The Window➪Arrange menu command opens the Arrange Windows dialog box, which lists the four window arrangement options. You can choose from the Tiled, Horizontal, Vertical, or Cascade radio button. Just select the one that you want, and click OK.

Remember: The arrangement option that you select applies to all open windows. To apply the option only to the active workbook, select the Windows of Active Workbook check box in the Arrange Windows dialog box.

Changing a Worksheet's Name

By default, Excel names its worksheets Sheet1, Sheet2, and so on. Providing more meaningful names helps you identify a particular sheet. To change a sheet's name, click the sheet tab to select that worksheet and use any of the following methods to rename it:

✔ Choose Format⇨Sheet⇨Rename from the menu bar.

✔ Double-click the sheet tab.

✔ Right-click the sheet tab, and choose Rename from the shortcut menu that appears.

Any of these methods selects the text in the tab. Just type the new sheet name directly on the tab.

Remember: Sheet names can be up to 31 characters long. Names can include spaces but not the following characters: [ ] (brackets); : (colon); / (slash); \ (backslash); ? (question mark); and * (asterisk).

Coloring a Worksheet Tab

Excel enables you to add a color to a worksheet tab. You can use this feature, for example, to quickly identify a specific worksheet by its color. To color a worksheet tab, follow these steps:

1. Select the worksheet tab that you want to color.

2. Use any of the following methods to open the Format Tab Color dialog box:

    • Choose Format⇨Sheet⇨Tab Color from the menu bar.

    • Right-click the sheet tab, and choose Tab Color from the shortcut menu that appears.

3. Select a color for the tab from the Tab Color palette area of the Format Tab Color dialog box.

4. Click OK.

To undo the tab color, follow the same procedure, click the No Color option in the Format Tab Color dialog box, and click OK.

Remember: If you select a tab that you color-code, the sheet name appears underlined with the color. If a tab displays a background color, it's not currently selected.

Copying a Worksheet

You can make an exact copy of a worksheet — and put the copy either in its original workbook or in a different workbook — in any of the following ways:

 ✔ Choose Edit⇨Move or Copy Sheet from the menu bar, or right-click the worksheet tab and select Move or Copy from the shortcut menu that appears. Either method opens the Move or Copy dialog box. Select the location for the copy in the To Book drop-down list box (to copy the sheet to a new or other open workbook) and/or the Before Sheet list box. Make sure that the Create a Copy check box is selected. Click OK to make the copy.

 ✔ Click the sheet tab, press Ctrl, and drag the sheet to its desired location in the workbook. As you drag, the mouse pointer changes to a small sheet with a plus sign on it. To use this method to copy a worksheet to another open workbook, you must first arrange the workbooks. **See also** "Arranging Windows Automatically," earlier in this part.

Remember: To copy a worksheet to a different workbook, both workbooks must be open.

If necessary, Excel changes the name of the copied sheet to make it unique within the workbook. If you copy a sheet by the name of Sheet1 to a workbook that already contains a Sheet1, for example, Excel changes the name of the copied sheet to Sheet1 (2). To change the name of a sheet, **see** "Changing a Worksheet's Name," earlier in this part.

Deleting a Worksheet

You can delete a worksheet in one of the following two ways:

⮞ Activate the sheet by clicking the sheet tab, and choose Edit⇨Delete Sheet from the menu bar.

⮞ Right-click the sheet tab, and choose Delete from the shortcut menu.

In either case, if the sheet you want to delete contains data (or if you delete all of the data on a sheet in the current session), Excel asks you to confirm the fact that you want to delete the sheet. Every workbook must contain at least one sheet, so if you try to delete the only sheet, Excel complains.

 To select multiple sheets to delete, press Ctrl while clicking the sheet tabs that you want to delete. To select a group of contiguous sheets, click the first sheet tab, press Shift, and then click the last sheet tab.

 After you delete a worksheet, it's gone for good. This operation is one of the few in Excel that you can't undo. You may want to save a workbook before deleting worksheets. Then, if you inadvertently delete a worksheet, you can revert to the saved version.

E-Mailing Worksheet Data

You can send part of your worksheet data as the body of an e-mail message from within Excel. Sending data as the body of a message is useful if you want recipients to get a range of data, a chart, or a PivotTable report rather than an entire workbook.

Remember: To send part of your worksheet data as the body of a message, you need Outlook 2000 or higher or Outlook Express 5 or higher.

Follow these steps to send part of your worksheet data as the body of an e-mail message:

1. Use either of the following methods to display the E-mail toolbar and information text boxes:

• Click the E-mail button on the Standard toolbar.

• Choose File⇨Send To⇨Mail Recipient from the menu bar.

Excel displays an E-mail toolbar and recipient information text boxes.

Note: If Excel displays an E-mail dialog box prior to displaying the E-mail toolbar, select the Send the current sheet as the message body radio button and click OK.

2. Enter the pertinent data for the recipient — that is, the e-mail address and subject — by using the To, Cc, Subject, and Introduction text boxes. You can use the Introduction text box, for example, to explain the contents of the data you send.

3. Select the sheet, range, chart, or PivotTable report data that you want to send.

   The E-mail toolbar Send button's name changes depending on your selection. If you select a range to send, for example, the name changes to Send this Selection. If you select a chart, the name changes to Send this Chart, and so on.

4. Click the Send button to send the data in the body of the e-mail message. After you click the send button, Excel removes the display of the E-mail toolbar and information boxes.

   You can toggle the on/off display of the E-mail toolbar and information boxes by clicking the E-mail button.

   Remember: The data sent in the message body is formatted in HTML. To view the message, recipients must use Outlook 98 or higher, Outlook Express 4.01 or higher, a Web browser, or an e-mail program that can read documents in HTML format.

Freezing Row or Column Titles

Many worksheets (such as budgets) are set up with row and column headings. As you scroll through such worksheets, you can easily get lost after the row and column headings scroll out of view. Excel provides a handy solution to alleviate this problem: freezing rows and/or columns.

To freeze entire rows or columns, follow these steps:

1. Move the cell pointer to the cell below the row that you want to freeze and to the right of the column that you want to freeze. Use the following steps to freeze various portions of the worksheet:

   • To freeze row 1 and column A, for example, move the cell pointer to cell B2.

   • To freeze rows only, move the cell pointer below the rows that you want to freeze in column A.

   • To freeze columns only, move the cell pointer to the right of the columns that you want to freeze in row 1.

2. Choose Window⇨Freeze Panes from the menu bar.

Excel inserts dark lines to indicate the frozen rows and columns. These frozen rows and columns remain visible as you scroll throughout the worksheet.

Remember: Excel freezes all rows above the row you select and all columns to the left of the column you select. Therefore, to freeze a single row and/or column only, you must put your row heading in row 1 and your column heading in column A.

To unfreeze the frozen rows or columns, choose Window⇨Unfreeze Panes from the menu bar. *See also* "Splitting Panes," later in this part.

Hiding and Unhiding a Worksheet

Hiding a worksheet is useful if you don't want others to see it or if you just want to get it out of the way. If a sheet is hidden, its sheet tab is also hidden.

To hide a worksheet, choose Format⇨Sheet⇨Hide from the menu bar. The active worksheet (or selected worksheets) is hidden from view.

Remember: Every workbook must have at least one visible sheet, so Excel doesn't allow you to hide all sheets in a workbook.

To unhide a hidden worksheet, follow these steps:

1. Choose Format⇨Sheet⇨Unhide from the menu bar. The Unhide dialog box appears, listing all hidden sheets.

2. Choose the sheet that you want to unhide, and click OK.

Moving a Worksheet

Sometimes, you may want to rearrange the order of worksheets in a workbook — or move a sheet to a different workbook.

First, select the sheet that you want to move by clicking the sheet tab. You can also move multiple sheets at once by selecting them: Press Ctrl while you click the sheet tabs that you want to move.

You can move a selected worksheet(s) in the following ways:

✔ Choose Edit⇨Move or Copy Sheet from the menu bar, or right-click the worksheet tab and select Move or Copy from the short-cut menu that appears. Either method opens the Move or Copy dialog box. Select the location for the copy in the To Book drop-down list box (to move the sheet to a new or other open work-book) and/or the Before Sheet list box. Make sure that the Create a Copy check box is deselected. Click OK to move the sheet.

✔ Click the sheet tab, and drag the sheet to its desired location in the workbook. As you drag, the mouse pointer changes to a small sheet, and a small arrow guides you. To use this method to move a worksheet to another open workbook, you must first arrange the workbooks. *See also* "Arranging Windows Automatically," earlier in this part.

Remember: If you move a worksheet to a workbook that already contains a sheet by the same name, Excel changes the name to make it unique. For example, If you move Sheet1 to a workbook that already has a Sheet1, Excel changes the name of the sheet you are moving to Sheet1 (2). To change the name of a sheet, *see* "Changing a Worksheet's Name," earlier in this part.

Protecting a Worksheet

Deleting a single formula in a worksheet often creates a ripple effect, causing other formulas to produce an error value or, even worse, incorrect results. You can circumvent such problems by locking the cells that you don't want to be modified and then protecting your worksheets from modification by following these steps:

1. Choose Tools➪Protection➪Protect Sheet from the menu bar.

The Protect Sheet dialog box appears.

2. Provide a password in the Protect Sheet dialog box, if you want.

- If you enter a password, you must reenter the password before the sheet can be unprotected.

- If you don't supply a password, anyone can unprotect the sheet.

3. In the Allow All Users of this Worksheet To list box, click the appropriate check boxes to select the elements that users can change after the sheet is protected.

4. Click OK.

Remember: By default, all cells or objects have their locked property turned on, which means that the cells or objects are locked when you protect the worksheet. Before protecting a worksheet, you normally want to unlock the input cells (the cells in which you enter data). You can lock or unlock a cell or object by choosing Format⇨Cells for cells or Format⇨AutoShape for drawing objects to display the Format dialog box, and checking or unchecking the Lock check box on the Protection tab.

You can't change a cell's locked status while the worksheet is protected. You must unprotect the sheet to make any changes and then protect it again. To remove protection from a protected sheet, choose Tools⇨Protection⇨Unprotect Sheet from the menu bar.

Publishing Your Worksheet Data to the Web

Web publishing is the process of placing your Excel data on a Web or intranet server as a Web page. In this process, you save your Excel data in HTML format. Because your data is in HTML format, users can view your data by using their Internet browsers. Excel provides several features that are designed to make the publishing process relatively painless.

You can publish your data in static or interactive form. If you publish your data in static form, users can only view the data. If you publish your data with *interactive functionality,* users can work with and manipulate the data within their browsers. Excel provides the following three types of interactive functionality:

- **Spreadsheet functionality:** If you publish your data with spreadsheet functionality, users can enter and calculate data, and format, sort, filter, or cut and paste data in the published sheet.

- **PivotTable functionality:** If you publish your data with Pivot-Table functionality, users can change the layout of a PivotTable and format, sort, filter, or cut and paste data in the published PivotTable.

- **Chart functionality:** If you publish your data with chart functionality, users can make changes to the source data (which is published with the chart) that automatically update the chart.

Publishing your worksheet data to a Web page

To publish worksheet data to a Web page, follow these steps:

1. Select the worksheet that contains the data that you want to put on a Web page.

2. Choose File⇨Save as Web Page from the menu bar.

3. In the Save As dialog box that appears, click the Publish button.

4. In the Publish as Web Page dialog box that appears, make a selection from the Choose drop-down list box. This list box provides the following three main selections:

   • **Previously published items:** Use this option to republish your data. *See* "Republishing your worksheet data to the Web," later in this part, for use of this option.

   • **Range of cells:** Use this option to publish a range of cells in your worksheet. This option is automatically selected for you if you select the range prior to Step 2 of this procedure.

   • **Items on *<Sheetname>*:** Use this option to publish items in *<Sheetname>*, where *<Sheetname>* is the name of the worksheet in which you want to publish the items. This option is automatically selected if you don't select a specific item on *<Sheetname>* prior to Step 2 of this procedure.

   • **Entire Workbook:** Use this option to publish the entire workbook to a Web page.

5. In the list box below the Choose drop-down list, select the range or worksheet item that you want to publish.

   If you select Items on *<Sheetname>* in Step 4, the selection box may display up to five items, depending on the objects in your worksheet. These items are Sheet (for example, all data), Chart, PivotTable, AutoFilter, and Print Area.

6. In the File Name text box, type the pathname and filename where you want to save your worksheet or worksheet items. Click the Browse button to help you locate the appropriate directory, folder, intranet, or Internet location.

   You may also check any or all of the following options prior to Step 7:

   • **Add Interactivity With:** Check this box to enable users to manipulate the data after you publish it. Select the appropriate functionality (spreadsheet, PivotTable, or chart, as applicable) from the list box.

   • **Change:** Click this button to add a title for the Web page.

- **File Name:** Enter a name and location for your Web page if they are different from the name and location of your workbook file.

- **Open Published Web Page in Browser:** Select this check box to view the Web page in your browser after you save or publish it.

- **AutoRepublish every time this workbook is saved:** Select this check box if you want Excel to republish your workbook every time the workbook is saved. Using this option ensures that the data in your published location is always up to date.

7. Click the Publish button.

If you select the sheet, range, chart, PivotTable, AutoFilter, or print area prior to choosing File➪Save as Web Page, you can skip the Publish as Web Page dialog box by clicking the Selection: <*Item*> radio button in the Save As dialog box. <*Item*> may be Sheet, Chart, PivotTable, AutoFilter, Print Area, or a range of cells. Most of the options in the Publish as Web Page dialog box are available to you, except Open Published Web Page in a Browser and AutoRepublish every time this workbook is saved.

Remember: If you select a worksheet that contains a chart and save or publish it with spreadsheet functionality, the chart isn't included on the Web page.

Remember: You sometimes can't view all the formatting options that are applied to your document if the file is open in a Web browser, because Excel embeds additional information that describes complex formatting options to the HTML file. Many browsers can't interpret this additional information.

Republishing your worksheet data to the Web

Republishing data enables you to easily update a Web page that you already put on the Web by using Excel. Republishing enables you to update the Excel data, publish the data to a new location, change whether the data is interactive, and change the title of the data.

To republish your data, follow these steps:

1. Open the Excel workbook file that contains the worksheet items that you previously saved as a Web page and want to update.

2. After you finish updating your data, choose File➪Save As Web Page from the menu bar.

3. In the Save As dialog box that appears, click the Publish button.

4. In the Publish as Web Page dialog box that appears, select Previously Published Items in the Choose drop-down list box.

5. In the list box that is immediately below the Choose drop-down list box, select the range or worksheet item that you want to republish.

6. To change the interactivity, title, or file location of your document, make the changes in the appropriate dialog boxes.

7. Click the Publish button.

Remember: To republish data by using this procedure, you must resave your Excel worksheet after each publishing (or republishing) session.

If you want to keep the data in your published location up to date but don't need to change the location or change any of the other publishing options, you can check the AutoRepublish every time this workbook is saved check box in the Publish as Web Page dialog box.

Splitting Panes

Splitting an Excel window into two or four panes enables you to view multiple parts of the same worksheet. This procedure is an alternative to creating multiple views of the workbook to accomplish the same task. *See also* "Creating Multiple Windows (Views) for a Workbook," in Part I.

Some of the key features of splitting panes are as follows:

✔ The Window⇨Split menu command splits the active worksheet into two or four separate panes.

✔ The split occurs at the location of the cell pointer.

✔ You can use the mouse to drag the pane and resize it.

✔ To remove the split panes, choose Window⇨Remove Split.

A faster way to split and unsplit panes is to drag either the vertical or horizontal split bar, as shown in the following figure. These split bars are standard elements of the Excel window and are located above and to the right of the vertical and horizontal scroll bars, respectively. To remove split panes by using the mouse, drag the pane separator all the way to the edge of the window or just double-click it.

See also "Freezing Row or Column Titles," earlier in this part.

Using Full-Screen View

If you want to see as much information as possible, Excel offers a full-screen view. Choose View⇨Full Screen from the menu bar, and Excel maximizes its window and removes certain elements (all toolbars and the Formula Bar area but not the menu bar and row and column headings). Choose View⇨Full Screen again or click the Close Full Screen button in the floating Full Screen toolbar to return to normal.

Zooming Worksheets

Excel enables you to scale the size of your worksheets from 10 percent to 400 percent. Using a low zoom percentage can help you get a bird's-eye view of your worksheet to see its layout. A high zoom percentage can help you decipher very small text.

The easiest way to change the zoom factor of the active worksheet is to use the Zoom Control on the Standard toolbar. Just click the arrow, and select the desired zoom factor from the drop-down list. Your screen transforms immediately. (You can also choose View⇨Zoom to open the Zoom dialog box or type a number directly into the Zoom text box on the Standard toolbar.)

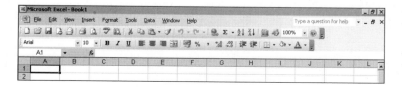

The Selection option in the toolbar's Zoom Control drop-down list zooms the worksheet to display only the selected cells. This option is useful if you want to view only a particular range. For finer control over the zoom factor, you can click the Zoom Control, enter a zoom factor, and press Enter.

If you have a Microsoft IntelliMouse or equivalent device, you can zoom in or out in a worksheet by pressing Ctrl while you roll the mouse wheel. Make sure that the Zoom on Roll with IntelliMouse option is selected in the Options dialog box. (Choose Tools⇨Options to open the dialog box, and click the General tab to find the option.)

Part III

Entering and Editing Worksheet Data

This part deals with two of the most common tasks that you're likely to perform on a daily basis in Excel: entering data into worksheet cells and editing (or changing) the data after you enter it.

In this part . . .

Copying Cells and Ranges

Copying cells is a very common spreadsheet operation, and several types of copying are possible. You can do any of the following:

✔ Copy one cell to another cell.

✔ Copy a cell to a range of cells. Excel copies the source cell to every cell in the destination range.

✔ Copy a range to another range.

✔ Copy multiple cells or ranges to another range.

Remember: Copying a cell normally copies the cell contents, its cell comment (if any), and the formatting that was applied to the original cell. If you copy a cell that contains a formula, the cell references in the copied formulas change automatically to relate to their new location.

Copying a cell to another cell or a range

To copy the contents of one cell to a range of cells, follow these steps:

1. Move the cell pointer to the cell that you want to copy.

2. Click the Copy button on the Standard toolbar. (You can also press Ctrl+C or choose Edit➪Copy from the menu bar.)

3. Select the cell or range that you want to hold the copy.

4. Click the Paste button on the Standard toolbar. (You can also press Ctrl+V or choose Edit➪Paste.)

After you apply the Paste command (by using any of the methods that we describe in this step), Excel displays the Paste Options *Smart Tag* next to the copied range. Clicking the Paste Options Smart Tag provides a list of alternative paste options — for example, you can decide to match the destination formatting (otherwise, Excel copies the source data formatting by default), copy formatting only (but not the data), and so on.

If you don't need to use any of the alternative options that are available in the Paste Options Smart Tag as you perform a copy operation, you can just press Enter. This action also automatically clears the copy operation.

5. Press Esc to clear the copy operation and remove the Paste Options Smart Tag.

Note: This step isn't necessary if you press Enter in Step 4.

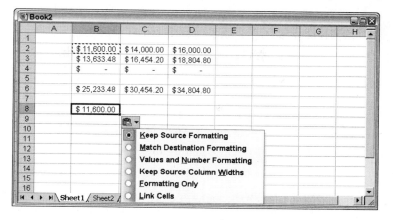

 If the range that you're copying to is adjacent to the cell that you're copying from, you can drag the cell's AutoFill handle to copy the cell to the adjacent range. *See also* "Filling a Series," later in this part.

Copying a range to another range

To copy the contents of one range to another range of the same size, follow these steps:

1. Select the range that you want to copy.

 2. Click the Copy button on the Standard toolbar. (You can also press Ctrl+C or choose Edit⇨Copy from the menu bar.)

3. Select the upper-left cell of the range that you want to hold the copy.

 4. Click the Paste button on the Standard toolbar. (You can also press Ctrl+V or choose Edit⇨Paste.)

Instead of using the Paste button, you can press Enter if you don't need to use any of the options in the Paste Options Smart Tag.

5. Press Esc to clear the copy operation and remove the Paste Options Smart Tag.

Note: This step isn't necessary if you press Enter in Step 4.

See also "Copying a cell to another cell or a range," earlier in this part.

 If the location that you're copying to isn't too far away, you can follow these steps:

1. Select the cell or range to copy.

2. Press and hold Ctrl.

3. Move the mouse pointer to any of the selection's borders.

   The mouse pointer changes to an arrow with a small plus sign.

4. Drag the mouse to the location where you want to copy the cell or range.

   Excel displays an outline of the range as you drag with the mouse to help you see where you're going to paste the range.

5. Release the mouse button.

   Excel copies the cell or range to the new location.

Remember: If the mouse pointer doesn't change to an arrow in Step 3, your drag-and-drop feature is off. To turn on the drag-and-drop feature, follow these steps:

1. Choose Tools⇨Options.

2. Click the Edit tab of the Options dialog box that appears.

3. Select the Allow Cell Drag and Drop check box.

4. To prevent accidental overwriting of data in destination range, select the Alert Before Overwriting Cells check box.

5. Click OK.

Copying data to another worksheet or workbook

To copy the contents of a cell or range to another worksheet or workbook, follow these steps:

1. Select the cell or range that you want to copy.

2. Click the Copy button on the Standard toolbar. (You can also press Ctrl+C or choose Edit⇨Copy.)

3. Click the tab of the worksheet that you're copying to.

   If the worksheet lies in a different workbook, activate that workbook (by selecting the workbook from the bottom part of the Window menu) and then click the tab of the worksheet that you want to hold the copied data.

4. Select the upper-left cell of the range that you want to hold the copy.

5. Click the Paste button on the Standard toolbar. (You can also press Ctrl+V or choose Edit⇨Paste.)

6. Press Esc to clear the copy operation and remove the Paste Options Smart Tag.

See also "Copying a cell to another cell or a range" and "Copying a range to another range," both earlier in this part.

Copying multiple cells or ranges to another range

To copy noncontiguous cells or ranges to a single range elsewhere in the worksheet, to a different worksheet in the same workbook, or to a range in a different workbook, you can copy and paste each cell or range in turn to the new range. However, Excel provides a simpler and less tedious method to perform this multiple-copy task. This method uses the *Office Clipboard* to copy multiple data items prior to pasting the items. The Office Clipboard differs from the *Windows Clipboard* in that the Windows Clipboard (which you use for copy-and-paste operations in most Windows applications) can store only one data item at a time.

The Office Clipboard can store 24 copied items. All Office applications share the Office Clipboard (and the 24-item limit), enabling you to cut and paste multiple items between Excel and other Office applications, such as Word and PowerPoint.

To copy multiple cells or ranges to another range, follow these steps:

1. Choose View⇨Task Pane or press Ctrl+F1 to display the task pane window.

2. If the task pane window isn't displaying the Clipboard task pane, click the down arrow in the Task Pane title bar and select Clipboard from the drop-down list.

3. Select the first cell or range that you want to copy. (*See* "Selecting Cells and Ranges," later in this part, for details.)

4. Click the Copy button on the Standard toolbar. (You can also press Ctrl+C or choose Edit➪Copy from the menu bar.)

   Excel copies the data to the Office Clipboard. The Clipboard task pane displays a portion of or all the copied data.

5. Select the next cell or range that you want to copy. (The cell or range can be from the same worksheet, another worksheet in the same workbook, or a worksheet in another open workbook.)

6. Repeat Steps 4 and 5 for all the remaining data that you want to copy.

7. Select the upper-left cell of the range that you want to hold the copied items.

8. Click the Paste All button in the Clipboard task pane.

   You can also click individual items in the Clipboard task pane to paste a single item at a time.

 You can enable the Office Clipboard by setting the Clipboard task pane to appear automatically after the second use of the Copy command. This option, if set, eliminates Steps 1 and 2. To turn on this option, click the Options button at the bottom of the Clipboard task pane and select the Show Office Clipboard Automatically check box.

 Normally, you need to display the Clipboard task pane to enable the Office Clipboard. If you prefer to use the Office Clipboard without displaying the Clipboard task pane, click the Options button at the bottom of the Clipboard task pane and select the Collect Without Showing Office Clipboard check box.

Remember: You can use the Office Clipboard for multiple cut operations in addition to the multiple copy operations that we discuss in this section.

Deleting Entire Rows and Columns

In certain circumstances, you may want to delete entire rows or columns from your worksheet. If you delete a row(s), the rows below the deleted row(s) shift upward to fill the gap. If you delete a column(s), the columns to the right of the deleted column(s) shift to the left to fill the gap.

To delete entire rows or columns, follow these steps:

1. Select a cell or range in the row(s) or column(s) that you want to delete. (*See* "Selecting Cells and Ranges," later in this part, for details.)

2. Choose Edit⇨Delete, right-click the selected row or column, and choose Delete from the shortcut menu, or Press Ctrl+– (the minus sign).

   Excel displays the Delete dialog box.

3. Select the Entire Row or Entire Column radio button.

4. Click OK.

You can also delete entire rows or columns by selecting those rows or columns first. Then use any of the methods in Step 2 to select the Delete command. Excel deletes the rows or columns without displaying the Delete dialog box. *See also* "Selecting entire rows and columns," later in this part.

Make sure that any cells that you want to keep aren't in the rows or columns you delete. You can zoom out in your worksheet to check for any cells that aren't normally visible on-screen. *See also* "Zooming Worksheets," in Part II.

Editing a Cell's Contents

After you enter information into a cell, you can edit it. To edit the contents of a cell, use one of the following ways to get into cell-edit mode:

- ✔ Double-click the cell to edit the cell contents directly in the cell.

- ✔ Click the cell and Press F2. This key enables you to edit the cell contents directly in the cell.

- ✔ Click the cell that you want to edit; then click the Formula Bar to edit the cell contents in the Formula Bar.

All these methods cause the Formula Bar to display two new mouse icons. The following table describes these icons and what they do.

Icon	*What It Does*
✗	Cancels editing, and the cell's contents don't change. (Pressing Esc has the same effect.)
✓	Confirms the editing and enters the modified contents into the cell. (Pressing Enter has the same effect.)

Remember: If nothing happens after you double-click a cell, or if pressing F2 puts the cursor in the Formula Bar instead of directly in the cell, the in-cell editing feature is turned off. To turn on in-cell editing, follow these steps:

1. Choose Tools➪Options.

2. Click the Edit tab of the Options dialog box that appears.

3. Select the Edit Directly in Cell check box.

If you're editing a cell that contains a formula, the Name Box (at the extreme left in the Formula Bar) displays a list of worksheet functions if you click the downward-pointing arrow next to the box. You can select a function from the list, and Excel provides assistance entering the arguments.

DATEVALUE		▾ X ✓ ƒ⨯ =A2*12	
A	B	C	D
1 =A2*12			
2 500			

If you're editing the contents of a cell (either directly in the cell or in the Formula Bar), the cursor changes to a vertical bar; you can move the vertical bar by using the direction keys. You can add new characters at the cursor's location. After you're in edit mode, you can use any of the following keys or key combinations to perform your edits:

- **Left/right arrow:** Moves the cursor left or right one character, respectively, without deleting any characters.

- **Ctrl+left/right arrow:** Moves the cursor one group of characters to the left or right, respectively.

- **Shift+left/right arrow:** Selects characters to the left or right of the cursor, respectively.

- **Shift+Home:** Selects from the cursor to the first character in the cell.

- **Shift+End:** Selects from the cursor to the last character in the cell.

- **Backspace:** Erases the character to the immediate left of the cursor.

- **Delete:** Erases the character to the right of the cursor or erases all selected characters.

- **Insert:** Places Excel in OVR (Overwrite) mode. Rather than adding characters to the cell, you *overwrite,* or replace, existing characters with new ones, depending on the position of the cursor.

- **Home:** Moves the cursor to the beginning of the cell entry.

  ✔ **End:** Moves the cursor to the end of the cell entry.

  ✔ **Enter:** Accepts the edited data.

Remember: If you change your mind after editing a cell, you can choose Edit⇨Undo from the menu bar (or press Ctrl+Z) to restore the cell's previous contents.

You also can use the mouse to select characters while you're editing a cell. Just click and drag the mouse pointer over the characters that you want to select.

Remember: If the cell is locked and the worksheet is protected, you can't make any changes to the cell unless you unprotect the worksheet (by choosing Tools⇨Protection⇨Unprotect Sheet).

See also "Protecting a Worksheet," in Part II.

Entering Data into a Range

Excel provides timesaving methods for you to enter data quickly in a range of cells. These methods are particularly helpful if you need to enter a lot of data manually.

Entering data into a specific range

If you're entering data into a range of cells, you may want to select the entire range of cells before you start entering data. This action causes Excel to move the cell pointer to the next cell in the selection after you press Enter.

The procedure works as follows:

  ✔ If the selection consists of multiple rows, Excel moves down the column; after it reaches the end of the column, it moves to the top of the next column.

  ✔ To skip a cell, press Enter without entering anything.

  ✔ To go backward, press Shift+Enter. If you prefer to enter the data by rows rather than by columns, press Shift+Tab.

You may find setting Excel to "speak" (read back audibly) the cells as you enter data useful. *See* "Proofreading Your Worksheet Data," in Part VI.

Entering the same data into a range of cells

If you need to enter the same data (value, text, or formula) into multiple cells, your first inclination may be to enter it once and then copy it to the remaining cells. The following steps show you a better way:

1. Select all the cells that you want to contain the data. (*See also* "Selecting a range," later in this part.)

2. Enter the value, text, or formula into one cell.

3. Press Ctrl+Enter.

   Excel inserts the single entry into each cell in the selection.

Entering Dates and Times

Excel treats a date or a time as a value — but you format it to appear as a date or a time. If you work with dates and times, you need to understand Excel's date and time system. Excel's system for working with dates uses a serial number system. The earliest date that Excel understands is January 1, 1900 (which has a serial number of 1). January 2, 1900, has a serial number of 2; January 1, 2004, has serial number of 37987; and so on. This system makes it easy to deal with dates in formulas.

Entering specific dates and times

Normally, you don't need to concern yourself with the Excel serial-number date system. You can simply enter a date in a familiar format, and Excel takes care of the details.

If you plan to use dates in formulas, make sure that the date you enter is one that Excel recognizes as a date (that is, a value); otherwise, your formula produces incorrect results. Excel is quite smart in recognizing dates that you enter into a cell, and it recognizes most common date formats. But it's not perfect. Excel interprets the following entries, for example, as text and not dates:

✔ June 1 2004

✔ Jun-1 2004

✔ Jun-1/2004

Remember: Excel uses a *windowing* approach for interpreting 2-digit year entries. That is, within a 100-year window, Excel interprets 1/1/29 as January 1, 2029. If you enter 1/1/30, Excel interprets it as January 1, 1930. To be safe, enter the year as a four-digit value and then format it as you want.

The best way to deal with times is to enter the time into a cell in a recognized format. The following table lists some examples of time formats that Excel recognizes.

Entered into a Cell	Excel's Internal Interpretation
11:30:00 am	11:30 a.m.
11:30:00 AM	11:30 a.m.
11:30 pm	11:30 p.m.
11:30	11:30 a.m.

You also can combine dates and times, as follows.

Entered into a Cell	Excel's Internal Interpretation
6/1/04 11:30	11:30 a.m. on June 1, 2004

Entering the current date or time

If you need to date-stamp or time-stamp a cell in your worksheet, Excel provides the following two shortcut keys that perform this task for you:

- **Current date:** Press Ctrl+; (semicolon)

- **Current time:** Press Ctrl+Shift+; (semicolon)

Entering Formulas

A *formula* is a special type of cell entry that returns a result: After you enter a formula into a cell, the cell displays the result of the formula. The formula itself appears in the Formula Bar (which is just below the toolbars at the top of the Excel window) after you activate the cell.

A formula begins with an equal sign (=) and can consist of any of the following elements:

- Operators, such as + (for addition) and * (for multiplication)

- Cell references, including addresses such as B4 or C12, as well as named cells and ranges

- Values and text

- Worksheet functions (such as SUM)

You can enter a formula into a cell in one of two ways: manually (by typing it in) or by pointing to cell references. *See also* "Basic Formula Essentials," in Part IV, for more information on operators and operator precedence.

Entering formulas manually

To enter a formula manually, follow these steps:

1. Move the cell pointer (by clicking the cell or navigating with the arrow keys) to the cell that you want to hold the formula.

2. Type an equal sign (=) to signal the fact that the cell contains a formula.

3. Type the formula and press Enter.

As you type, the characters appear in the cell as well as in the Formula Bar. You can use all the normal editing keys (Delete, Backspace, direction keys, and so on) in entering a formula.

As you enter a formula, Excel shows each cell reference in the formula in a different color. If the reference cells are visible on the worksheet, you see a border around each cell in the same color as the cell reference in the formula. This feature makes it easier to identify the references of the cells that you're typing in your formulas.

See also "Entering formulas by pointing," immediately following in this part.

Entering formulas by pointing

The pointing method of entering a formula still involves some manual typing. The advantage is that you don't need to type the cell or range references. Instead, you point to them in the worksheet, which is usually more accurate and less tedious.

The best way to explain this procedure is with an example. Follow these steps to enter the formula =A1/A2 into cell A3 by using the pointing method:

1. Move the cell pointer to cell A3 (by clicking the cell or navigating with the arrow keys).

   This cell is where you want the formula (and the result) to go.

2. Type an equal sign (=) to begin the formula.

3. Press the up-arrow key twice.

   As you press this key, notice that Excel displays a moving border around the reference cell (A1) and that the cell reference appears in cell A3 and in the Formula Bar.

DATEVALUE	▾ X ✓ ƒₓ	=A1	
	A	B	C	D
1	$12,000.00			
2				
3	=A1			

Excel colors the cell reference in the formula and the moving border around the reference cell (A1) with the same color.

4. Type a division sign (/).

    Excel now displays a solid colored border around the A1 cell reference.

5. Press the up-arrow key once.

    Excel adds A2 to the formula.

    Excel now displays a different color for the new cell reference in the formula and the same color for the border of the new reference cell.

6. Press Enter to end the formula entry.

See also "Entering formulas manually," earlier in this part.

Entering Text

You can use text in worksheets to serve as labels for values and headings for columns, or to provide instructions about the worksheet. An entry of mixed text and numbers is still considered text. A cell can hold as many as 32,767 characters.

Entering text into cells

To enter text (rather than a value or a formula) into a cell, follow these steps:

1. Move the cell pointer to the appropriate cell (by clicking the cell or navigating with the arrow keys).

2. Type the text.

3. Press Enter or any of the direction keys.

If you enter text that's longer than its column's current width, one of the following two things happens:

✔ If the cells to the immediate right are blank, Excel displays the text in its entirety, spilling the entry into adjacent cells.

✔ If an adjacent cell isn't blank, Excel displays as much of the text as possible. (The cell contains the full text; it just doesn't display all of it.)

In either case, you can always see the text that you're typing because it appears in the Formula Bar as well as in the cell. After you enter the text, you can always see all of your entry in the Formula Bar, even if it appears cut off in the cell.

Remember: To display a long text entry that's adjacent to a cell with an entry, you can edit your text to make it shorter, increase the width of the column, or wrap the text within the cell so that it occupies more than one line.

See also "Wrapping text within a cell" and "Modifying Cell Size," both in Part VII.

If you have lengthy text in a cell, you can force Excel to display it in multiple lines within the cell. Press Alt+Enter to start a new line in a cell. When you add this line break, Excel automatically changes the cell's format to Wrap Text.

See also "Wrapping text within a cell," in Part VII.

Completing text entries by using AutoComplete

AutoComplete enables you to type the first few letters of a text entry into a cell, and Excel automatically completes the entry based on other entries that you've already made in the column. Your column entries must be contiguous (that is, have no blank cells between entries). AutoComplete doesn't work with entries in a row.

AutoComplete works with no effort on your part; just follow these steps:

1. Begin entering text or a value.

If Excel recognizes your entry, it automatically completes it.

2. If Excel guesses correctly, press Enter to accept it. To enter something else, just continue typing and ignore Excel's guess.

You also can access this feature by right-clicking the cell and choosing Pick from List from the shortcut menu. If you use this method, Excel displays a drop-down list of all the entries in the current column. Just click the one that you want, and Excel enters it automatically.

If you don't like the AutoComplete feature, you can turn it off in the Edit tab of the Options dialog box. (Choose Tools➪Options to display the Options dialog box.) Just deselect the Enable AutoComplete for Cell Values check box and click OK.

Remember: AutoComplete works only with pure text or mixed text (text and values); it doesn't work with pure values.

Entering Values

Values, also known as numbers, represent a quantity of some type: revenue, number of units, test scores, and so on. Values can stand on their own, or you can use the values that you enter into cells as part of a formula or in creating a chart. Excel's numbers are precise up to 15 significant digits. If you enter a larger number, Excel stores it with only 15 digits of precision.

Entering values into cells

To enter a numeric value into a cell, follow these steps:

1. Move the cell pointer to the appropriate cell (by clicking the cell or navigating with the arrow keys).

2. Enter the value.

3. Press Enter or any of the direction keys.

The value displays in the cell, and it also appears in the Excel Formula Bar. You can also include a decimal point, dollar sign, plus sign, minus sign, and comma. If you precede a value with a minus sign or enclose it in parentheses, Excel considers the value a negative number.

Remember: Sometimes the value doesn't appear exactly as you enter it. Excel may convert very large numbers to scientific notation. The Formula Bar always displays the value that you originally entered.

Entering fractions

To enter a fraction into a cell, leave a space between the whole number part and the fractional part. To enter the decimal equivalent of 6⅞, for example, follow these steps:

1. Type **6**.

2. Type a space.

3. Type **7/8**.

4. Press Enter.

   Excel enters 6.875 into the cell and automatically formats the cell as a fraction. ***See also*** "Formatting Numbers," in Part VII.

If the value has no whole number part (for example, ⅛), you must enter a zero and a space first, as follows: **0 1/8** — otherwise, Excel interprets the entry as January 8 of the current year.

Erasing Data in Cells and Ranges

To erase the contents of a cell but leave the cell's formatting and cell comments intact, perform the following two steps:

1. Select the cell or range that you want to erase. (**See** "Selecting Cells and Ranges," later in this part, for details.)

2. Press Delete.

For more control over what you delete, you can select Edit⇨Clear. This menu item leads to a submenu that contains the following four additional choices:

✓ **All:** Clears everything from the cell.

✓ **Formats:** Clears only the formatting and leaves the value, text, or formula.

✓ **Contents:** Clears only the cell's contents and leaves the formatting.

✓ **Comments:** Clears the comment (if one exists) that is attached to the cell.

Filling a Series

Excel provides the AutoFill feature, which enables you to fill in several types of data series in a row or column. AutoFill uses the fill handle — the small square that appears at the bottom-right corner of the selected cell or range.

Excel provides an AutoFill Options *Smart Tag* next to the fill handle after you drag the fill handle to a new location. Click the AutoFill Options Smart Tag to display a list of commonly used fill options, such as Copy Cells, Fill Series, Fill Formatting Only, and Fill Without Formatting.

Remember: If the selected cell or range doesn't have a fill handle, it means that this feature is turned off. To turn on AutoFill, follow these steps:

1. Chose Tools⇨Options.

2. Click the Edit tab.

3. Select the Allow Cell Drag and Drop check box, and click OK.

Remember: You can't use AutoFill if you make a multiple selection.

Entering a series of incremental values or dates

To use AutoFill to enter a series of incremental values, follow these steps:

1. Enter at least two values or dates in the series into adjacent cells. These values need not be consecutive.

2. Select the cells that you used in Step 1. (*See* "Selecting a range," later in this part, for details.)

3. Click and drag the fill handle to complete the series in the cells that you select.

   As you drag the fill handle, Excel displays a small box that tells you what it's planning to enter into each cell.

Remember: After you complete the drag operation, Excel displays the Auto Fill Options Smart Tag. You can click the Smart Tag to select a different fill option. For even more control, drag the fill handle while pressing the right mouse button. After you release the button, you see a list of options.

 AutoFill also works in the negative direction. If you use AutoFill by starting with two cells that contain −20 and −19, for example, Excel fills in −18, −17, and so on.

 If the values in the cells that you enter don't have equal increments, Excel completes the series by calculating a simple linear regression. This feature is handy for performing simple forecasts. *Note:* Excel calculates a simple linear regression or progression, depending on the direction (negative or positive) of the series.

Entering a series of text

Excel is familiar with some text series (days of the week, months of the year), and it can complete these series for you automatically.

Follow these steps to use AutoFill to complete a known series of text:

1. Enter any of the series into a cell (for example, **Monday** or **February**).

2. Click and drag the fill handle to complete the series in the cells that you select.

You can also teach Excel to recognize custom series. Choose Tools⇨Options, and click the Custom Lists tab of the Options dialog box that appears. The Custom Lists list box displays all series that Excel recognizes. Click the NEW LIST option, and enter your list in the List Entries text box. Click Add to store the list. Your custom list also works with AutoFill. *See also* "Using a custom sort order," in Part XI.

Inserting Decimal Points Automatically

If you're entering lots of numbers with a fixed number of decimal places, you can save some time by having Excel enter the decimal point. (This feature is similar to the feature that is available on some adding machines and office calculators.) To do so, follow these steps:

1. Choose Tools⇨Options from the menu bar.

2. Click the Edit tab of the Options dialog box that appears.

3. Select the Fixed Decimal check box, and set the number of decimal places that you want to use by clicking the Places spinner control.

4. Click OK.

Excel subsequently supplies the decimal points for you automatically. If you have it set for two decimal places and you enter **12345** into a cell, for example, Excel interprets it as 123.45. (It adds the decimal point.) To restore things to normal, just deselect the Fixed Decimal check box in the Options dialog box.

Remember: Changing this setting doesn't affect any values that you've already entered.

Inserting Entire Rows and Columns

If you insert new rows or columns in Excel, the program places blank rows or columns in the worksheet, and surrounding rows or columns move out to accommodate the new rows or columns.

To insert new rows or columns in your worksheet, follow these steps:

1. Select a cell or range in the row(s) or column(s) in which you want to insert new row(s) or column(s). (**See** "Selecting Cells and Ranges," later in this part, for details.)

2. Choose Insert⇨Cells, right-click the cell or range and choose Insert from the shortcut menu, and press Ctrl+Shift+ + (the plus sign on the top row of keys) or Ctrl+ + (the plus sign on the numeric keypad).

   Excel displays the Insert dialog box.

3. Select the Entire Row or Entire Column radio button.

4. Click OK.

You can also insert entire rows or columns by selecting the entire rows or columns first. Then use any of the methods in Step 2 to choose the Insert command. Excel deletes the rows or columns without displaying the Insert dialog box. **See also** "Selecting entire rows and columns," later in this part.

Moving Cells and Ranges

Moving the data in a cell or a range is common. You may, for example, need to relocate a range of data to make room for something else.

Moving data to a new location in the same worksheet

Follow these steps to move a cell or range:

1. Select the cell or range to move. (**See** "Selecting Cells and Ranges," later in this part, for details.)

2. Choose Edit⇨Cut.

   You can also press Ctrl+X or click the Cut button on the Standard toolbar.

3. Move the cell pointer to the range that you want to hold the copy (by clicking the cell or navigating with the arrow keys). You need to select only the upper-left cell in the range.

4. Press Enter.

If the range that you're moving contains formulas that refer to other cells, the references continue to refer to the original cells. You almost always want references to continue to refer to the original cells.

If the location that you're moving to isn't too far away, you can follow these steps:

1. Select the cell or range to move. (*See* "Selecting Cells and Ranges," later in this part.)

2. Move the mouse pointer to any of the selection's borders.

The mouse pointer changes to an arrow with a small directional cross at its tip.

3. Drag the mouse to the location where you want to move the cell or range.

4. Release the mouse button.

Excel moves the cell or range to the new location.

If you press and hold Shift while dragging, Excel performs a move and an insert paste in a single operation, without use of the Insert dialog box.

Remember: If you change your mind after Step 2, press Esc to cancel the operation. If you change your mind after you move the data, choose Edit⇨Undo Paste or press Ctrl+Z.

Remember: If the mouse pointer doesn't change to an arrow in Step 2, your drag-and-drop feature is off. To turn on the drag-and-drop feature, follow these steps:

1. Choose Tools⇨Options from the menu bar.

2. Click the Edit tab of the Options dialog box that appears.

3. Select the Allow Cell Drag and Drop check box.

4. To prevent accidental overwriting of data in destination range, select the Alert Before Overwriting Cells check box.

5. Click OK.

If you move data, make sure that you have enough blank cells to hold it. Excel overwrites existing data without warning.

Moving data to a different worksheet or workbook

If you want to move the contents of a cell or range to a different worksheet or to a different workbook, follow these steps:

1. Select the cell or range to move. (*See* "Selecting Cells and Ranges," later in this part, for details.)

2. Select Edit⇨Cut.

You can also press Ctrl+X or click the Cut button on the Standard toolbar.

3. Activate the worksheet that you're moving to by clicking the sheet tab. If you're moving the selection to a different workbook, activate that workbook and then activate the worksheet. (Select the workbook from the bottom part of the Window menu.)

4. Move the cell pointer to the range that you want to hold the copy (by clicking the cell or navigating with the arrow keys). You only need to select the upper-left cell in the range.

5. Press Enter.

After you move data, make sure that you have enough blank cells to hold it. Excel overwrites existing data without warning.

Remember: If you change your mind after Step 2, press Esc to cancel the operation. If you change your mind after you move the data, choose Edit⇨Undo Paste or press Ctrl+Z.

Replacing the Contents of a Cell

To replace the contents of a cell with something else, follow these steps:

1. Select the cell. (*See* "Selecting a cell," later in this part, for details.)

2. Type your new entry. (It replaces the previous contents.)

Remember: Any formatting that you applied to the cell remains.

Searching and Replacing Data

If your worksheets contain lots of data, you may find locating a particular piece of information difficult. A quick way to do so is to have Excel find it for you. Sometimes you may need to replace all occurrences of a value or text with something else. Excel also makes this task easy to do.

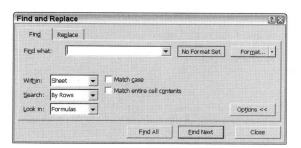

Searching for data

To locate a particular value or sequence of text, follow these steps:

1. Choose Edit⇨Find or press Ctrl+F.

   Excel displays its Find and Replace dialog box. The Find tab is automatically selected.

2. In the Find What drop-down list box, enter the characters to search for. You can also use the Find What drop-down list box to select items that you previously searched for.

   To make your search case-sensitive, select the Match Case check box. If the Match Case check box isn't visible, click the Options button.

3. To search for data with specific formatting, click the Format button; otherwise, skip to Step 5. If the Format button isn't visible, click the Options button.

   Excel displays the Find Format dialog box.

4. Select the appropriate tabs, and in each tab, specify the formatting that you're looking for. After you complete your selections, click OK to exit the Find Format dialog box.

   If a cell in your worksheet contains the target formatting, click the Choose Format From Cell button. Excel adds a "dropper" icon to the cursor. Click the cell with the target formatting.

5. In the Within drop-down list box, select whether you want to look in the active sheet or the entire workbook.

   If the Within drop-down box isn't visible, click the Options button.

6. In the Search drop-down box, select the direction that you want to search, as follows:

   • Select By Rows to search across rows.

   • Select By Columns to search down columns.

   In most cases, your search goes faster if you select By Columns.

7. In the Look In drop-down list box, specify what to look in: Formulas, Values, or Comments.

8. Click the Find Next button. Excel selects the cell that contains what you're looking for.

   If you click the Find All button, Excel displays a drop-down window that shows all references to the found data, either in the active worksheet or across the entire workbook, depending on your selection in Step 5. Click a reference in the window to go directly to that cell.

9. Click the Close button to end your search.

For approximate searches, use *wildcard characters.* An asterisk represents any group of characters in the specified position, and a question mark represents any single character in the specified position. If you type **w*h**, for example, those letters represent all text that begins with *w* and ends with *h.* Similarly, **b?n** matches three-letter words such as *bin, bun,* and *ban.*

Remember: To find a cell or cells with specific formatting but containing no specific data, you can skip Step 2.

See also "Searching for and replacing data," immediately following in this part.

Searching for and replacing data

To replace all occurrences of a value or text with something else, follow these steps:

1. Choose Edit➪Replace or press Ctrl+H.

Excel displays its Find and Replace dialog box. The Replace tab is automatically selected.

2. In the Find What drop-down list box, enter the text or value to search for.

3. To search for data with specific formatting, click the Format button to the right of the Find What drop-down list box; otherwise, skip to Step 5. If the Format button isn't visible, click the Options button.

Excel displays the Find Format dialog box.

4. Select the appropriate tabs, and in each tab, specify the formatting that you're looking for. After you complete your selections, click OK to exit the Find Format dialog box.

If a cell in your worksheet contains the target formatting, click the Choose Format From Cell button. Excel adds a "dropper" icon to the cursor. Click the cell with the target formatting.

5. In the Replace With drop-down list box, enter the text or value to replace the text or value from Step 2.

6. To specify new formatting for the replaced characters, click the Format button to the right of the Replace With drop-down list box and follow the procedure that we outline in Step 4; otherwise, skip to Step 7.

7. In the Within drop-down list box, select whether you want to look in the active sheet or the entire workbook for the information that you typed in Step 2.

   If the Within drop-down box isn't visible, click the Options button.

8. Click the Replace All button to have Excel search and replace all occurrences automatically.

   To verify each replacement, click the Find Next button. Excel pauses after it finds a match. To replace the found text, click Replace. To skip it and find the next match, click the Find Next button again. Click the Find All button to select a match from the drop-down window.

9. Click the Close button after you finish finding and replacing the text.

See also "Searching for data," earlier in this part.

Selecting Cells and Ranges

In Excel, you normally select a cell or range before performing an operation that works with the cell or range. Topics in this section describe how to make various types of cell and range selections.

Selecting a cell

To select a cell (and make it the active cell), use any of the following techniques:

- ✔ Move the cell pointer to the cell by using the arrow keys.

- ✔ Click the cell with the mouse.

- ✔ Select Edit⇨Go To (or press F5 or Ctrl+G), enter the cell address in the Reference text box of the Go To dialog box that appears, and click OK.

The selected cell now has a dark border around it, and its address appears in the Name Box.

Selecting a range

You can select a range in any of the following ways:

- ✔ Click the mouse in a cell and drag to highlight the range. If you drag to the end of the screen, the worksheet scrolls.

- ✔ Move to the first cell of the range. Press F8, and then move the cell pointer with the direction keys to highlight the range. Press F8 again to return the arrow keys to normal movement.

✔ Press Shift as you use the arrow keys to select a range.

✔ Choose Edit⇨Go To (or press F5), enter a range's address in the Reference text box of the Go To dialog box that appears, and click OK.

Selecting noncontiguous ranges

Most of the time, the ranges that you select are *contiguous* — they are a single rectangle of cells. Excel also enables you to work with noncontiguous ranges, which consist of two or more ranges (or single cells) that aren't necessarily next to each other (also known as a *multiple selection*).

To apply the same formatting to cells in different areas of your worksheet, one approach is to make a multiple selection. After you select the appropriate cells or ranges, Excel applies the formatting that you choose to all the selected cells. The following figure shows two non-contiguous ranges (B2:F2 and B6:F6) that have been selected.

	A	B	C	D	E	F
1		January	February	March	April	May
2	Celery	200	150	500	350	150
3	Cauliflower	225	540	400	325	140
4	Okra	450	220	330	410	270
5	Artichoke	75	160	400	300	270
6	Broccoli	125	85	240	150	390
7	Total	1075	1155	1870	1535	1220
8						

Book2 — Sheet1 / Sheet2 / Sheet3

You can select a noncontiguous range in any of the following ways:

✔ Press and hold Ctrl as you click the mouse and drag to highlight the individual cells or ranges.

✔ From the keyboard, select a range by pressing F8 and then use the arrow keys. After selecting the first range, press Shift+F8, move the cell pointer using the arrow keys, and press F8 to start selecting another range.

✔ Select Edit⇨Go To (or press F5 or Ctrl+G), and enter a range's address in the Reference text box of the Go To dialog box that appears. Separate the different ranges with a comma. Click OK, and Excel selects the cells in the ranges that you specify.

Selecting entire rows and columns

You can select entire rows or columns in any of the following ways:

✔ Click the row or column heading to select a single row or column.

✔ To select multiple adjacent rows or columns, click a row or column heading and drag to highlight additional rows or columns.

✔ To select multiple (nonadjacent) rows or columns, press Ctrl as you click the row or column headings that you want.

✔ Press Ctrl+spacebar to select the column of the active cell or the columns of the selected cells.

✔ Press Shift+spacebar to select the row of the active cell or the rows of the selected cells.

✔ Click the Select All button (or press Ctrl+Shift+spacebar) to select all rows. Selecting all rows is the same as selecting all columns, which is the same as selecting all cells.

Selecting a multisheet (3-D) range

An Excel workbook can contain more than one worksheet, and a range can extend across multiple worksheets. You can think of these as three-dimensional ranges.

To select a multisheet range, follow these steps:

1. Select the range on the active sheet. (*See* "Selecting a range," earlier in this part, for details.)

2. Press Ctrl, and click the sheet tabs of the other sheets to include in the selection.

Notice that the workbook's title bar displays [Group]. This display is a reminder that you selected a group of sheets and that you're in Group Edit mode. The range that you select is also selected on each sheet in the group.

After you select a multisheet range, you can perform the same operations that you can perform on a single sheet range.

If the multisheet range consists of a contiguous worksheet, you can press Shift and then click the tab of the last sheet that you want to include. Pressing Shift selects all sheets from the active sheet up to and including the sheet that you click.

Transposing a Range

If you need to change the orientation of a range, Excel can do it for you in a snap. If you transpose a range, rows become columns and columns become rows.

The following figure shows an example of a horizontal range that we transposed to a vertical range.

	A	B	C	D	E	F	G
1							
2	Jan	Feb	Mar	Apr	May	Jun	
3	450	489	522	512	566	602	
4							
5							
6		Jan	450				
7		Feb	489				
8		Mar	522				
9		Apr	512				
10		May	566				
11		Jun	602				
12							

To transpose a range, follow these steps:

1. Select the range to transpose. (**See** "Selecting a range," earlier in this part, for details.)

2. Choose Edit⇨Copy (or press Ctrl+C or click the Copy button on the Standard toolbar).

3. Click the upper-left cell where you want the transposed range to go.

   The transposed range can't overlap the original range.

4. Choose Edit⇨Paste Special.

5. Select the Transpose check box in the Paste Special dialog box that appears.

6. Click OK.

7. Delete the original range, if necessary.

Remember: Excel adjusts any formulas in the original range so that they work correctly after you transpose them.

Undoing Changes and Mistakes

One very useful feature in Excel is its multilevel Undo feature. This feature means that you can reverse your recent actions, one step at a time. If you discover that you accidentally deleted a range of data several minutes ago, for example, you can use the Undo feature to "backtrack" through your actions until the deleted range reappears.

Remember: You can undo your actions only in a sequential manner. In other words, if you want to undo an action, you must also undo all the actions that you performed after the action that you want to undo. You can undo as many as the past 16 operations that you performed.

To undo an operation, use any of the following techniques:

- ✔ Choose Edit⇨Undo. The command tells you what you're undoing.

- ✔ Press Ctrl+Z or Ctrl+Backspace until you arrive at the action that you want to undo.

- ✔ Click the Undo button on the Standard toolbar until you arrive at the action that you want to undo.

- ✔ Click the arrow on the Undo button on the Standard toolbar. This action displays a description of your recent actions. Select the actions that you want to undo.

Validating Data Entry

You can specify the type of data that a cell can accept. If you develop a spreadsheet that others use, for example, you can limit the range of values that a user may enter into input cells. Excel then validates the user input to ensure that the values the user enters fall within the range that you specify. Excel displays an error message if a user enters an invalid value.

To specify data-entry validation criteria, follow these steps:

1. Select the cell or range that you want to validate. (*See* "Selecting Cells and Ranges," earlier in this part, for details.)

2. Choose Data⇨Validation.

   Excel displays the Data Validation dialog box.

3. Click the Settings tab, and specify the type of data that the cell is to have by selecting an entry from the Allow drop-down list box and the Data drop-down list box, if applicable.

   To limit the entry in a cell to whole numbers between 100 and 200, for example, select Whole Number in the Allow drop-down list box, select Between in the Data drop-down box, enter **100** in the Minimum text box, and enter **200** in the Maximum text box.

4. To specify a message to appear after a user clicks an input a cell, click the Input Message tab and type a message in the Input Message text box. If you want a title to appear at the top of the message, enter a title in the Title text box.

   Following the example that we gave in Step 3, you can type the message **Enter a value between 100 and 200**, which appears after the user clicks the cell.

5. To specify a custom error message to appear in a dialog box if someone enters invalid data, click the Error Alert tab and type

a message in the Error Message text box. If you want a title to appear at the top of the message, enter a title in the Title text box.

Following the example that we gave in Step 3, you can type the message **Please enter a value between 100 and 200**, which appears in a dialog box if the user enters invalid data in a cell.

6. Choose a style for the error message from the Style drop-down list box (Stop, Warning, or Information). Each style that you select displays an error icon and various buttons on the error dialog box as follows:

   • **Stop:** Displays Retry and Cancel buttons.

   • **Warning:** Displays Yes, No, and Cancel buttons. (Clicking Yes enters the invalid data.)

   • **Information:** Displays OK and Cancel buttons. (Clicking OK enters the invalid data.)

7. Click OK.

If you subsequently want to remove the validation criteria from a cell or range, select the cell or range, choose Data⇨Validation, and click the Clear All button in the Data Validation dialog box that appears.

Remember: If you don't specify a message in Step 5, Excel uses a default message if a data-entry error occurs.

 Remember: Using this technique isn't foolproof. The validation doesn't occur if the user pastes invalid data into a cell that's validated. However, you can flag this type of error by choosing Tools⇨Formula Auditing⇨Show Formula Auditing Toolbar and clicking Circle Invalid Data on the Formula Auditing toolbar that appears.

Part IV

Using Formulas and Functions

This part deals with topics that are related to formulas and functions. Formulas make using spreadsheets valuable by allowing you to calculate results from data stored in the worksheet. Functions are built-in or custom tools that are used in formulas. They can make your formulas perform powerful feats and save you a great deal of time.

In this part . . .

Absolute, Relative, and Mixed References

An *absolute reference* uses two dollar signs in its address, one for the column part and one for the row part. If you copy a formula containing an absolute reference, Excel doesn't adjust the reference in the copied cell. On the other hand, Excel adjusts *relative references* as you copy the formula.

Excel also enables you to use *mixed references,* in which only one of the address's parts is absolute. The following table summarizes all the possible types of cell references.

Example	Type
A1	Relative reference
A1	Absolute reference
$A1	Mixed reference (column part is absolute)
A$1	Mixed reference (row part is absolute)

To change the type of cell reference in a formula, follow these steps:

1. Double-click the cell containing the formula (or press F2) to get into Edit mode.

2. In the Formula Bar, click the mouse pointer on the cell reference.

3. Press F4 repeatedly to cycle through all possible cell reference types. Stop after the cell reference displays the correct type.

4. Press Enter to complete the operation.

Add-In Functions

Some functions are available only if a particular add-in is open. (An *add-in* is a file that you load into Excel to provide additional commands or worksheet functions. In addition to the add-ins that ship with Excel 2003, you can create your own or install add-ins that a third party supplies.) To use add-in worksheet functions, follow these steps:

1. Choose Tools⇨Add-Ins from the menu bar to open the Add-Ins dialog box.

2. In the Add-Ins Available list box, click the check box next to the add-in that contains the functions that you need.

3. Click OK.

You can then use the add-in functions in your formulas.

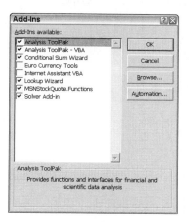

If the add-in that you want to use isn't yet installed, it doesn't appear in the Add-Ins Available list box. To install the add-in, click the Browse button in the Add-Ins dialog box to open the Browse dialog box. In the Look In drop-down box, navigate to the location of the add-in file that you want. (Add-in files use the XLA or XLL file extension.) Double-click the filename or click OK to install the add-in.

Remember: If you attempt to use an add-in function before you load the add-in, the formula displays #NAME?.

Basic Formula Essentials

A formula can consist of up to 1,024 characters and any of the following elements:

- ✔ Operators such as + (for addition) and * (for multiplication)
- ✔ Cell references (including named cells and ranges)
- ✔ Values, text, or logical values
- ✔ Worksheet functions (such as SUM or AVERAGE)

After you enter a formula into a cell, the cell displays the result of the formula. You see the formula itself in the *Formula Bar* as the cell activates. (The Formula Bar lies immediately below the Formatting toolbar.)

Operator precedence is the set of rules that Excel uses to perform its calculations in a formula.

The following table provides the list of operators that you can use in formulas and indicates the operators' precedence.

Operator	Name	Precedence
^	Exponentiation (raised to a power)	1
*	Multiplication	2
/	Division	2
+	Addition	3
–	Subtraction	3
&	Concatenation (joins text)	4
=	Equal to	5
>	Greater than	5
<	Less than	5

The table shows that exponentiation has the highest precedence (that is, Excel performs it first), and logical comparisons have the lowest precedence. If two operators have the same precedence, Excel performs the calculations from left to right.

Remember: You can override operator precedence by using parentheses in your formulas. In the formula =**(Income–Expenses)** *** TaxRate**, for example, Expenses are subtracted from Income, and the result is multiplied by TaxRate.

Changing When Formulas Are Calculated

If the Excel calculation mode is set to Automatic (the default setting), changing cells that you use in a formula causes the formula to display a new result automatically.

To set the Excel calculation mode to Manual, follow these steps:

1. Choose Tools⇨Options from the menu bar.

Excel displays the Options dialog box.

2. Click the Calculation tab.

3. Click the Manual option button.

4. Click OK.

If you switch to Manual calculation mode, Excel automatically turns on the Recalculate Before Save check box. You can turn this option off if you want to speed file-save operations.

Remember: If you're working in Manual calculation mode, Excel displays Calculate in the status bar if you have any uncalculated formulas. Use the following shortcut keys to recalculate the formulas:

✔ **F9:** Calculates the formulas in all open workbooks.

✔ **Shift+F9:** Calculates only the formulas in the active worksheet. Other worksheets in the same workbook aren't calculated.

Remember: The Excel calculation mode isn't specific to a particular worksheet. If you change the calculation mode, that change affects all open workbooks and not just the active workbook.

Converting Formulas to Values

Sometimes, you may want to convert a formula to its current value (remove the formula and leave only its result). You may, for example, want to prevent future changes to the value of a cell if other cells that the formula references change.

To convert a formula to its current value, follow these steps:

1. Select the cell that contains the formula. To convert several formulas, you can select a range.

 2. Choose Edit⇨Copy from the menu bar. (You can also press Ctrl+C or click the Copy button on the Standard toolbar.)

3. Choose Edit⇨Paste Special.

4. In the Paste Special dialog box that appears, select the Values option button.

5. Click OK.

6. Press Enter to cancel Copy mode.

Remember: The preceding procedure overwrites the formulas. To put the current values of the formulas in a different (empty) area of the worksheet, select a different range before Step 3 in the preceding list.

Editing Functions in Formulas

After you create a formula with one or more functions, you may later want to modify the arguments in one of the functions. Excel provides several ways for you to modify a function. The method that you choose depends on personal choice and the complexity of the function.

Use any of the following techniques to modify a function:

 ✔ If your formula contains only one function or if the function you want to modify is the last one in the formula, click the Insert Function button on the Formula Bar or press Shift+F3 to display the Function Arguments dialog box for the function.

✔ If your formula contains more than one function, press F2 or double-click the formula cell. Position the cursor within the function that you want to modify and click the Insert Function button, or press Shift+F3.

✔ The most efficient way to modify simple functions (that is, those with few arguments) is to do so manually. Excel 2003 provides a ToolTip for the function to help you identify the names and order of the function's arguments.

See also "Entering Functions in Formulas," immediately following in this part.

Entering Functions in Formulas

Excel provides more than 300 built-in functions that can make your formulas perform powerful feats and save you a great deal of time.

Functions perform the following tasks:

✔ Simplify your formulas

✔ Enable formulas to perform calculations that are otherwise impossible

✔ Enable "conditional" execution of formulas — giving them some rudimentary decision-making capability

Most, but not all, worksheet functions use one or more arguments, enclosed in parentheses. Think of an argument as a piece of information that clarifies what you want the function to do. For example, the following function (which rounds the number in cell A1 to two decimal places) uses two arguments:

```
=ROUND(A1,2)
```

Remember: You can *nest* a function within another function. The formula =SUM(MAX(B1:B6),ROUND(A1,2)), for example, nests the MAX and ROUND functions within the SUM function.

See also "Editing Functions in Formulas," immediately preceding in this part.

Entering functions manually

If you're familiar with the function that you want to use, you may choose to simply type the function and its arguments into your formula. Often, doing so is the most efficient method.

Remember: If you're using a function at the beginning of a formula, you must provide an initial equal sign (=).

As you enter a function, Excel always converts it to uppercase. A good idea is to use lowercase letters in entering functions: If Excel doesn't convert the function to uppercase, it doesn't recognize your entry as a function. (You probably spelled it incorrectly.)

Excel provides you with assistance as you enter a function. This assistance enables you to determine the number and order of arguments in the function. Excel displays a *ScreenTip* (pop-up text in a box) below the function that you're typing after you enter the function name followed by an open parenthesis. The ScreenTip includes the name of the function that you typed followed by the names of all the function's mandatory and optional arguments in parentheses. To display a Help window for the function, click the function name in the ScreenTip.

Using the Extended AutoSum tool

The *Extended AutoSum tool* provides a quick method for you to enter some functions that you commonly use.

To use the Extended AutoSum tool, follow these steps:

1. Click a cell below or to the right of a range of numbers.

2. Perform one of the following actions:

- To sum the range, click the AutoSum button in the Standard toolbar.

   Excel places a *marquee* around cells that it thinks you want to sum. If the range of cells that the marquee surrounds isn't the range that you want to sum, use the mouse to highlight a new range. Click the AutoSum button again or press Enter to complete the operation.

- To find the average, count, minimum, or maximum of the range, click the arrow on the AutoSum button to display a menu for selecting these operations. Click the operation that you want to perform from the menu, and follow procedure that we describe for summing the range after Excel places the marquee around the cells.

- To access additional functions, click the arrow on the AutoSum button and select More Functions from the menu that pops up. Excel displays the Insert Function dialog box, from which you can select a function. **See also** "Using the Insert Function dialog box," immediately following in this part.

Excel automatically places a marquee around the first region that it encounters above or to the left of the formula cell. A *region* is a range that contains nonblank cells. To select multiple regions as

you use the AutoSum tool in Step 2, press and hold Ctrl while dragging the mouse over each region. **See also** "Selecting Cells and
Ranges," in Part III.

Using the Insert Function dialog box

The Insert Function dialog box enables you to easily enter a function and its arguments. Using this tool ensures that you spell the
function correctly and that it has the correct number of arguments
in the correct order. The Insert Function dialog box is an enhanced
version of the Paste Function dialog box that previous versions of
Excel used.

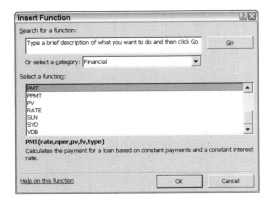

To enter a function by using the Insert Function dialog box, follow
these steps:

1. Activate the cell that is to contain the function. If you're inserting the function into an existing formula, click the formula at
   the position where you want to insert the function.

2. If you're inserting a new function adjacent to another function
   in a formula, you must add an operator (for example, +, −, *, /,
   and so on) at this point to delimit the two functions.

3. Use any of the following four methods to open the Insert
   Function dialog box:

   • Choose Insert⇨Function from the menu bar.

   • Click the Insert Function button on the Formula Bar.

   • Press Shift+F3.

   • Click the arrow next to the AutoSum button, and select
     More Functions from the drop-down list that appears.

4. In the Insert Function dialog box, select a function category from the Or Select a Category drop-down list box and choose the function that you want from the Select a Function list box.

Excel displays the Function Arguments dialog box. The Function Arguments dialog box prompts you for each argument of the function that you select. You can enter the arguments manually or (if they're cell references) point to them in the worksheet. The Function Arguments dialog box displays the result.

5. After you specify all the required arguments, click OK.

To get help with the function, click the Help on this Function link in the Insert Function dialog box. Excel displays the Help window for the function.

Excel provides a quick method of inserting functions that you used recently. Instead of completing Steps 3, 4, and 5 of the preceding list, after Step 2, click the arrow next to the Functions drop-down list box to display a list of recently used functions. (The Functions drop-down list box appears on the left side of the Formula Bar, where the Name text box normally resides.) Selecting a function in the list opens the Function Arguments dialog box. Selecting More Functions at the bottom of the list opens the Insert Function dialog box.

The Insert Function dialog box provides a search option, which enables you to find a function if you're unsure of the function's name. The Search for a Function text box prompts you on how to use this feature. Excel displays a list of functions that match the description that you type into the Search for a Function text box.

Modifying a Range Reference Used in a Function

If you edit a cell that contains a formula, Excel color-codes the references in the formula and places an outline around each cell or range that the formula references. The color of the outline corresponds to the color that appears in the formula. Each outlined cell or range also contains *fill handles* (a small square in each corner of the outlined cell or range).

If your formula contains a function that uses a range argument, you can easily modify the range reference by following these steps:

1. To begin editing the formula, press F2 or double-click the cell.

If double-clicking the cell doesn't work, you need to turn on the option to enable direct cell editing. To turn on the option, choose Tools➪Options, click the Edit tab in the Options dialog box that appears, and select the Edit Directly in Cell check box.

2. Locate the range that the function uses. (The range appears with an outline.)

3. Drag a fill handle to extend or contract the range. You can also click a border of the outlined range and move the outline to a new range. In either case, Excel changes the range reference in the formula.

4. Press Enter.

Remember: Formulas that contain name references place a colored outline around the named cell or range. The outline doesn't provide fill handles, however, or enable you to move this type of reference by clicking a border of the outline.

	A	B	C	D	E	F
1						
2	Jan	587		=AVERAGE(B2:B7)		
3	Feb	817				
4	Mar	835				
5	Apr	467				
6	May	588				
7	Jun	272				
8	Jul	582				
9						

Book1 — Sheet1 / Sheet2 / Sheet3

Referencing Cells in Other Worksheets

If your formula needs to refer to a cell in a different worksheet in the same workbook, use the following format for your formula:

```
SheetName!CellAddress
```

Precede the cell address with the worksheet name, and follow it with an exclamation point.

Remember: If the worksheet name in the reference includes one or more spaces, you must enclose it in single quotation marks. The following is a formula that refers to a cell on a sheet by the name of All Depts:

```
=A1*'All Depts'!A1
```

See also "Linking Workbooks," in Part X.

Part V

Creating and Using Names

Dealing with cryptic cell and range addresses can sometimes be confusing. Fortunately, Excel enables you to assign descriptive names to cells and ranges. You can give a cell a name such as *InterestRate,* for example, or you can name a range *JulySales.*

In this part . . .

Using names for cells and ranges offers the following advantages:

- ✔ A meaningful range name (such as `Total Income`) is much easier to remember than a cell address (such as AC21).

- ✔ You can quickly move to areas of your worksheet by using the Name Box, located at the left side of the Formula Bar (by clicking the arrow to open a drop-down list of defined names), or by choosing Edit⇨Go To from the menu bar (or pressing F5) and specifying the range name.

- ✔ After you select a named cell or range, its name appears in the Name Box.

- ✔ Creating formulas is easier. You can paste a cell or range name into a formula by choosing Insert⇨Name⇨Paste or by selecting a name from the Name drop-down list box.

- ✔ Names make your formulas more understandable and easier to use. `=Income-Taxes` is more intuitive than `=D20-D40`.

- ✔ Macros are easier to create and maintain if you use range names rather than cell addresses.

Although Excel is quite flexible about the names that you can define, it does have the following rules:

- ✔ Names must begin with a letter or the underscore character (_).

- ✔ Names can't contain any spaces. You may want to use an underscore or a period character to simulate a space (such as `Annual_Total` or `Annual.Total`).

- ✔ You can use any combination of letters and numbers, but the name must not begin with a number (such as `3rdQuarter`) or look like a cell reference (such as `Q3`).

- ✔ You can't use most symbols. You can, however, use the underscore (_), period (.), backslash (\), and question mark (?).

- ✔ Names can be no more than 255 characters long.

- ✔ You can use single letters (except for R or C), but we don't recommend this practice because it defeats the purpose of using meaningful names.

Remember: A cell or range can have more than one name; you can't, therefore, override the name of a cell or range merely by typing in a new name. ***See also*** "Changing Names," immediately following in this part.

Excel also reserves a few names internally for its own use. Avoid using the following for names: `Print_Area`, `Print_Titles`, `Consolidate_Area`, and `Sheet_Title`.

Changing Names

Excel doesn't offer a simple way to change a name after you create it. If you create a name and then realize that it's not the name you want (or perhaps, that you spelled it incorrectly), you can change the name by following these steps:

1. Create the new name by using any of the techniques that we describe in the following section of this part.

2. Delete the old name.

See also "Deleting Names" and "Creating Names," later and immediately following in this part, respectively.

Creating Names

Excel provides several useful methods for creating names. The method or methods that you choose to create names depend on personal preference and techniques that may allow you to save time.

Creating names by using the Define Name dialog box

To create a range name by using the Define Name dialog box, follow these steps:

1. Select the cell or range that you want to name.

2. Choose Insert➪Name➪Define from the menu bar (or press Ctrl+F3).

   Excel opens the Define Name dialog box.

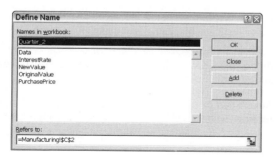

3. Type a name in the Names in Workbook text box (or use the name that Excel proposes, if any).

The active or selected cell or range address appears in the Refers To text box.

4. Verify that the address Excel lists is correct. To refer to a different address, either type the new cell or range address in the Refers To text box (with a leading equal sign) or delete the address in the Refers To text box and then use the mouse pointer to select the cell or range on the worksheet.

5. Click OK to close the dialog box.

You can also click the Add button to continue adding names to your worksheet. If you do so, you must specify the Refers To range by typing an address (making sure that you begin the name with an equal sign) or by pointing to it in the worksheet. Each name that you add then appears in the list box.

Creating names by using the Name Box

The Name Box is at the left side of the Formula Bar. To create a name by using the Name Box, follow these steps:

1. Select the cell or range to name.

2. Click the Name Box, and enter the name.

3. Press Enter to create the name.

Remember: If a name already exists, you can't use the Name Box to change the reference for the name. Attempting to do so simply displays the already existing name.

Creating names automatically

Your worksheet may contain text that you want to use for names of adjacent cells or ranges. You may have sales region names in column A, for example, and corresponding sales figures in column B. You can create a name for each cell in column B by using the text in column A.

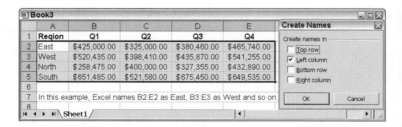

To create names by using adjacent text, follow these steps:

1. Select the name text and the cells that you want to name. (These can be individual cells or ranges of cells.)

   The names must be adjacent to the cells that you're naming. (A multiple selection isn't possible here.)

2. Choose Insert⇨Name⇨Create from the menu bar (or press Ctrl+Shift+F3).

   The Create Names dialog box appears. Excel guesses how to create the names by selecting the appropriate Create Names In check boxes. If the text is on the left of the cells that you want to name, for example, Excel selects the Left Column option.

3. If Excel's selection isn't what you want, select or deselect the correct Create Names In check boxes (as necessary) to correspond to the manner in which you want to create the names.

4. Click OK to create the names.

Remember: If the text that a cell contains results in an invalid name, Excel modifies the name to make it valid. If Excel encounters a value or a formula where text should be, however, it doesn't convert it to a valid name. It simply doesn't create a name.

Remember: The names that you create do *not* include the cells with the name text.

Creating multisheet names

Names can extend into the third dimension — across multiple worksheets in a workbook. Multisheet names must include contiguous worksheets and must refer to the same cell or range reference in each worksheet. To create a multisheet name, follow these steps:

1. Choose Insert⇨Name⇨Define from the menu bar to open the Define Name dialog box.

2. Enter the name in the Names in Workbook text box in the Define Name dialog box.

3. Enter the reference in the Refers To text box (and remember to begin it with an equal sign). The format for a multisheet reference is as follows:

   ```
   FirstSheet:LastSheet!RangeReference
   ```

4. Click OK.

Remember: This name doesn't appear in the Name box, however, or in the Go To dialog box. Excel allows you to define the name, but it doesn't give you a way to automatically select the cells to which the name refers.

An easier way to enter the reference in Step 3 is by pointing. Follow these steps after Step 2 (of the preceding list) to create a multi-sheet reference by pointing:

1. Click the Refers To text box, and delete the suggested reference (which usually isn't the one you want).

2. Select the cell or range in the first worksheet that you want to include in the name reference.

   If the first worksheet in the reference isn't active, click its tab and then select the cell or range.

3. Press and hold Shift, and click the tab of the last worksheet that you want to include in the reference.

4. Click OK.

Creating a Table of Names

You may want to create a list of all names in the workbook. This procedure may be useful for tracking down errors or as a way to document your work.

To create a table of names, follow these steps:

1. Move the cell pointer to an empty area of your worksheet. (Excel creates the table at the active cell position.)

2. Choose Insert⇨Name⇨Paste from the menu bar (or press F3).

3. Click the Paste List button in the Paste Name dialog box that appears, and Excel creates your table of names at that spot.

The list that Excel pastes overwrites any cells that get in the way, so make sure that the active cell is in an empty portion of the worksheet.

Deleting Names

If you no longer need a defined name, you can delete it by following these steps:

1. Choose Insert⇨Name⇨Define from the menu bar.

2. In the Define Name dialog box that appears, select the name that you want to delete from the list.

3. Click the Delete button.

4. Click OK.

Be extra careful in deleting names. If you use the name in a formula, deleting the name causes the formula to become invalid. (Excel displays #NAME?.) Even worse, you can't undo the deletion of a name. A good practice, therefore, is to save your workbook before you delete any names.

If you delete the rows or columns that contain named cells or ranges, the names contain an invalid reference. For example, if cell A1 on Sheet1 is named Interest and you delete row 1 or column A, Interest then refers to =Sheet1!#REF! (that is, an erroneous reference). If you use the name Interest in a formula, the formula displays #REF.

Names in Formulas

At the beginning of this part, we discuss several advantages of using names in formulas. You should make a conscious effort to use names in your formulas (and descriptive ones at that). Thankfully, Excel provides several techniques that make the task of applying names to formulas relatively painless.

Applying names to existing cell references

If you create a new name for a cell or a range, Excel doesn't automatically use the name in place of existing references in your formulas. If you have a formula such as =A1*20 and then give a name to cell A1, for example, the formula continues to display A1 (not the new name). Replacing cell or range references with their corresponding names, however, is fairly easy.

To apply names to cell references in existing formulas, follow these steps:

1. Select the range that you want to modify.

2. Choose Insert⇨Name⇨Apply.

3. In the Apply Names dialog box that appears, select the names that you want to apply by clicking them.

   To select multiple contiguous names, click the first name, press and hold Shift, and select the last name. To select multiple noncontiguous names, click the first name, press and hold Ctrl, and select the other names.

4. Click OK.

   Excel replaces the range references with the names in the selected cells.

If you select a nonformula cell in Step 1, Excel applies the names to all formulas in the worksheet.

Pasting names into a formula

If your formula uses named cells or ranges, you can type the name in place of the address. A less error-prone approach is to choose the name from a list and have Excel insert the name for you automatically. You can do so in either of the following two ways:

✔ Choose Insert⇨Name⇨Paste. Excel displays its Paste Name dialog box with all the names listed. Select the name, and click OK.

✔ Press F3. This command also opens the Paste Name dialog box.

Using row and column headers

You can take advantage of the fact that Excel recognizes row and column headers. You can use these headers to make your formulas more legible. Use the worksheet shown in the following figure as a reference. (This workbook doesn't have any defined names.)

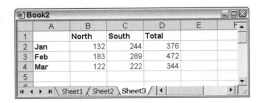

To refer to a particular cell in this table, you can use the row and column headers (separating them with a space). The following formula, for example, returns 289:

```
=Feb South
```

If you get the #NAME? error instead of the value you expect, the feature isn't turned on. To turn on the feature, choose Tools⇨Options and click the Calculation tab. Select the Accept Labels in Formulas check box and click OK.

Remember: This technique works only for formulas that are on the same sheet as the table.

Using sheet-level names

Normally, you can use a name that you create anywhere within the workbook. Names, by default, are *book-level* names rather than *sheet-level* names. But what if you have several worksheets in a workbook and you want to use the same name (such as Dept_Total) in each sheet to signify different values? You then need to create sheet-level names.

To define a sheet-level name, follow these steps:

1. Activate the worksheet where you want to define the name.

2. Choose Insert⇨Name⇨Define from the menu bar.

Excel displays the Define Name dialog box.

3. In the Names in Workbook text box, enter the name but precede it with the worksheet name and an exclamation point (for example, **Sheet2!Dept_Total**).

4. In the Refers To text box, enter the cell or range to which the name refers.

5. Click OK.

 You also can create a sheet-level name by using the Name Box. Select the cell or range, click the Name Box, and enter the name, preceding it with the sheet's name and an exclamation point.

Remember: If you write a formula that uses a sheet-level name on the sheet where you define it, you don't need to include the worksheet name in the range name. (The Name Box doesn't display the worksheet name either.) If you use the name in a formula on a different worksheet, however, you must use the entire name (sheet name, exclamation point, and name).

Naming Constants

Names that you use in Excel don't need to refer to a cell or a range. You can give a name to a constant. If formulas in your worksheet refer to an interest rate (such as .085, or 8.5 percent), for example, you can define a name for this particular constant and then use it in your formulas.

To define a name for a constant, follow these steps:

1. Choose Insert⇨Name⇨Define from the menu bar (or press Ctrl+F3).

Excel displays the Define Name dialog box.

2. Type the name for the constant in the Names in Workbook text box (or use the name that Excel proposes, if any).

3. In the Refers To text box, enter the value for the constant. Normally, this field holds a cell or range reference, but you can enter a value (or even a formula) in this text box.

4. Click OK to close the dialog box.

After performing these steps, you can use the name in your formulas.

Redefining Name References

After you define a name, you may want to change the cell or range to which it refers. To do so, follow these steps:

1. Choose Insert⇨Name⇨Define from the menu bar.

2. In the Define Name dialog box that appears, select the name whose reference you want to change from the list.

3. Edit the cell or range address in the Refers To text box.

   If you want, you can delete the address in the Refers To text box and select a new cell or range by pointing in the worksheet.

4. Click OK.

Auditing Your Work

When your worksheets begin to get larger and more complex, ensuring accuracy becomes more difficult. That's why, for all but the most basic spreadsheets, auditing is an important task. *Auditing* refers to the process of tracking down and identifying errors in your worksheet.

In this part . . .

Excel provides a set of interactive auditing tools that you may find helpful. You can access these tools by choosing Tools⇨Formula Auditing from the menu bar (which results in a submenu with additional choices) or from the Formula Auditing toolbar. (To display the Formula Auditing toolbar, choose Tools⇨Formula Auditing⇨Show Formula Auditing Toolbar.)

The tools on the Formula Auditing toolbar are as follows:

 Error Checking: Checks for particular errors in your worksheet — for example, formulas that are inconsistent with neighboring formulas, formulas that produce an error value, text dates with two-digit years, and so on.

 Trace Precedents: Draws arrows to indicate a formula cell's precedents. (A *precedent cell* supplies the values in a formula.) You can click this tool multiple times to see additional levels of precedents.

 Remove Precedent Arrows: Removes the most recently placed set of precedent arrows.

 Trace Dependents: Draws arrows to indicate a cell's dependents. (A *dependent cell* is a formula cell that depends on another cell.) You can click this tool multiple times to see additional levels of dependents.

 Remove Dependent Arrows: Removes the most recently placed set of dependent arrows.

 Remove All Arrows: Removes all precedent and dependent arrows from the worksheet.

 Trace Error: Draws arrows from a cell that contains an error to the cells that may have caused the error.

 New Comment: Inserts a Cell Comment for the active cell. This tool obviously doesn't have much to do with auditing — it just enables you to attach a comment to a cell.

 Circle Invalid Data: Draws a circle around cells that contain invalid data. These are cells that contain validation criteria that you set by choosing Data⇨Validation.

 Clear Validation Circles: Removes the circles from cells that contain invalid data.

 Show Watch Window: Displays a window that enables you to view cell formulas and values if the cells are out of view.

Evaluate Formula: Displays a dialog box that enables you to evaluate (check the current value of) parts of a formula.

Cell Comments

The Excel Cell Comment feature enables you to attach a comment to a cell. This is useful if you need to document a particular value, or it can help you to remember what a formula does. After you move the mouse pointer over a cell that has a comment, the comment appears in a small box.

Adding a cell comment

To add a comment to a cell, follow these steps:

1. Select the cell.

2. Choose Insert⇨Comment (or press Shift+F2).

   Excel displays a text box that points to the cell.

3. Enter the text for the comment into the text box.

4. Click any cell after you finish.

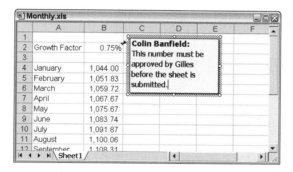

The cell displays a small red triangle to indicate that the cell contains a comment.

Editing a cell comment

To edit a cell comment, select the cell that contains the comment and then choose Insert⇨Edit Comment, press Shift+F2, or right-click and choose Edit Comment from the shortcut menu.

Changing the looks of a cell comment

You can change the looks of any cell comment by following these steps:

1. Select the cell that contains the comment.

2. Choose Insert⇨Edit Comment (or press Shift+F2).

   Excel displays a text box that points to the cell.

3. Double-click the comment's border to display the Format Comment dialog box.

4. Make your changes by clicking the appropriate tabs (Font, Colors and Lines, Alignment, and so on) and selecting the options that you want in each tab.

5. Click OK.

Viewing cell comments

Cells to which you attach a comment display a small red triangle in the upper-right corner. After you move the mouse pointer over a cell that contains a comment, Excel displays the comment.

To view the comments in all cells, choose View⇨Comments. Select View⇨Comments again to remove the comment display.

Checking for Specific Worksheet Errors

Excel can alert you of specific types of errors or potential errors in your worksheet. Excel can flag the following types of errors:

- ✔ Formulas that evaluate to error values (for example, #DIV/0!, #VALUE!, #N/A, and so on)

- ✔ Text dates (that is, dates that you format as text or precede with an apostrophe) that you enter with two-digit years

- ✔ Numbers that you store as text (that is, numbers that you format as text or precede with an apostrophe)

- ✔ Inconsistent formulas in a region (that is, different from formulas in surrounding cells)

- ✔ Formulas that omit cells in a region (for example, a formula that sums a range but omits the last cell or cells in the range)

- ✔ Unlocked cells that contain formulas if the worksheet is protected

- ✔ Formulas that contain references to cells that are empty

Remember: Use Excel's suggestions to serve as a guide only to alert you of potential errors in your worksheet, because Excel may flag some of the data that you enter (intentionally) as errors.

Excel's error-alert feature isn't foolproof. You should use it in conjunction with other techniques that we discuss in this part.

Checking for errors in the background

By default, Excel checks for worksheet errors in the background. If it identifies an error or potential error, Excel displays an indicator in the upper-left corner of the offending cell. After you click the cell, Excel displays the Error Warning tool on the left side of the offending cell. If you hover the mouse pointer over the Error Warning tool, Excel displays a message that indicates the nature of the error.

Dep-budg.xls						
	A	B	C	D	E	F	G
1		Quarter 1	Quarter 2	Quarter 3	Quarter 4		
2	Salaries	$375,000.00	$375,000.00	$525,000.00	$525,000.00		
3	Travel	$ 3,200.00	$ 4,500.00	$ 6,500.00	$ 4,500.00		
4	Supplies	$ 25,000.00	$ 26,000.00	$ 27,500.00	$ 28,000.00		
5	Facility	$ 13,500.00	$ 15,000.00	$ 15,000.00	$ 15,000.00		
6	Total	$403,200.00	$420,500.00	$574,000.00	$572,500.00		
7		The formula in this cell refers to a range that has additional numbers adjacent to it.					
8							
9							

Operations / Manufacturing

To correct or to tell Excel to ignore the error, click the Error Warning tool and select an option from the drop-down list that appears.

See also "Checking for errors manually," immediately following in this part.

Checking for errors manually

You may want to avoid the distraction of Excel's automatic worksheet error checking and perform the error-checking task manually after you complete work on your spreadsheet model.

To turn off background error checking, choose Tools⇨Options, click the Error Checking tab in the Options dialog box that appears, and deselect the Enable Background Error Checking check box.

To check for worksheet errors manually, follow these steps:

1. Select the worksheet that you want to check for errors.

2. Click the Error Checking button on the Formula Auditing toolbar.

   Excel displays the Error Checking dialog box and places the cell pointer in the first cell that it encounters containing an error or potential error. The dialog box indicates the nature of the error that you encounter in the cell.

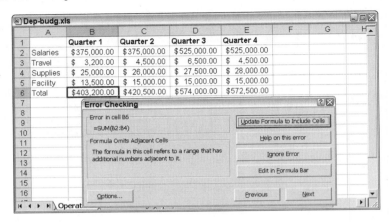

3. Click one of the four option buttons on the right side of the dialog box. (For a full discussion of the Show Calculation Steps button, **see** "Evaluating Parts of a Formula," later in this part.)

4. Click Next to move to the next cell that contains an error or potential error.

 An alternative to the procedure that we describe in the preceding steps is to turn on background error checking *after* your spreadsheet model is complete and use the procedure that we describe in "Checking for errors in the background," immediately preceding this section, for each cell that Excel flags with an error.

 You can control the types of errors that you want Excel to consider (automatically or via the manual procedure). Choose Tools➪Options, click the Error Checking tab in the Options dialog box that appears, and select or deselect the options in the Rules area.

Displaying Formulas in a Worksheet

One way to audit your workbook is to display the formulas rather than the results of the formulas. Then you can examine the formulas without needing to scroll through the worksheet.

To display formulas instead of the formula results (values), choose Tools➪Formula Auditing➪Formula Auditing Mode [or press Ctrl+~ (that is, the Ctrl/tilde sign shortcut-key combination)].

 You may want to create a new window for the workbook before issuing this command. That way, you can see the formulas in one window and the results in the other. **See also** "Creating Multiple Windows (Views) for a Workbook," in Part I.

Evaluating Parts of a Formula

Excel provides an Evaluate Formula tool that helps you to evaluate parts of a formula (that is, calculate the result) and to trace the precedents of the parts of the formula. The capability to evaluate parts of a formula can prove very useful if you're tracking down errors in formulas.

To evaluate parts of a formula, follow these steps:

1. Click the cell that contains the formula.

2. Choose Tools⇨Formula Auditing⇨Evaluate Formula.

 You can also click the Evaluate Formula button on the Formula Auditing toolbar.

Excel displays the Evaluate Formula dialog box. In the Reference area, the cell reference appears. The Evaluation preview box displays the formula with the first expression or cell reference underlined.

3. To show the value of the underlined expression, click Evaluate.

Excel italicizes the result of the expression.

4. Repeat Step 3 as many times as necessary to evaluate all expressions in the formula.

5. Use the Step In button to examine the formula that the underlined cell reference in the expression represents. Use the Step Out button to evaluate the current reference and return to the previous reference.

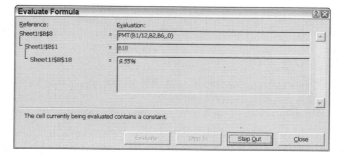

6. Click Close after you finish evaluating the formula.

Remember: The Step In button is not available if a cell reference lies in a different workbook.

A quick way to evaluate parts of a formula is to go into Edit mode (by double-clicking the cell or pressing F2), highlight the part of the formula that you want to evaluate, and press F9. Excel displays the result of the formula part. Press Esc to cancel. Do *not* press Enter; otherwise, Excel permanently replaces the part of the formula with the resulting value.

Formula Error Values

Excel flags errors in formulas with a message that begins with a pound sign (#). This flag signals that the formula is returning an error value. You must correct the formula (or correct a cell that the formula references) to get rid of the error display.

Remember: If the entire cell is full of pound signs, the column isn't wide enough to display the value.

The following table lists the types of error values that may appear in a cell that contains a formula.

Error Value	Explanation
#DIV/0!	The formula is trying to divide by zero (an operation that's not allowed on this planet). This error also occurs if the formula attempts to divide by an empty cell.
#NAME?	The formula uses a name that Excel doesn't recognize. This error can happen if you delete a name that the formula uses or if you have unmatched quotes when using text.
#N/A	A complete discussion of all the possible causes of this error is beyond the scope of this part. The error will occur, for example, if the formula refers (directly or indirectly) to a cell that uses #N/A or the NA() function to signal that data is not available. The error might also appear if a required argument is omitted from a worksheet function.
#NULL!	The formula uses an intersection of two ranges that don't intersect.
#NUM!	You have a problem with a value; for example, you're specifying a negative number where Excel expects a positive number.
#REF!	The formula refers to a cell that isn't valid. This error can happen if you've deleted the cell from the worksheet.
#VALUE!	The formula contains a function with an invalid argument, or the formula uses an operand of the wrong type (such as text where Excel expects a value).

Remember: A single error value can make its way to lots of other cells that contain formulas that depend on the cell.

See also "Tracing formula error values," later in this part.

Handling Circular References

As you enter formulas, you may occasionally see a message from Excel that is similar to the one shown in the following figure. This message indicates that the formula you just entered is going to result in a circular reference.

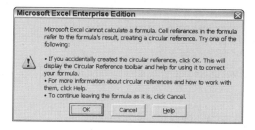

A *circular reference* occurs if a formula refers to its own value (either directly or indirectly).

If you get the circular reference message after entering a formula, Excel displays a message that enables you to correct the formula or to enter the formula as is. If you enter a formula with a circular reference, Excel displays a message in the status bar to remind you that a circular reference exists. Most of the time, a circular reference indicates an error that you must correct.

To locate the cells in the circular reference, use the Circular Reference toolbar. This toolbar contains a drop-down list that helps you move to each cell in the circular reference so that you can change the formulas as necessary to correct the error. Excel displays the Circular Reference toolbar (and a Help window) automatically if you click OK in the dialog box that displays the message about the circular reference.

Excel doesn't tell you about a circular reference if the Iteration setting is on. You can check this setting in the Calculation tab of the Options dialog box. (Choose Tools➪Options from the menu bar, and click the Calculation tab of the Options dialog box that appears.) If Iteration is on, Excel performs the circular calculation the number of times that the Maximum Iterations text box specifies (or until the value changes by less than 0.001 — or whatever value is in the Maximum Change text box).

Remember: A few situations exist (known about by advanced users) in which you use a circular reference intentionally. In these cases, the Iteration setting must be on. You're best off, however, keeping the Iteration setting off so that Excel warns you of circular references.

Locating Errors by Selecting Special Cells

The Go To Special dialog box can prove useful because it enables you to specify cells of a certain type that you want to select. You can, for example, select all the cells in the worksheet that contain formulas. (Excel highlights all such cells.) If Excel doesn't select a cell in a region where it highlights other cells (for example, a formula row or column), that situation may indicate that you inadvertently overwrote the cell with a value.

Follow these steps to select cells that meet your criterion:

1. Choose Edit➪Go To (or press F5 or Ctrl+G).

Excel displays the Go To dialog box.

2. Click the Special button in the Go To dialog box.

Excel displays the Go To Special dialog box.

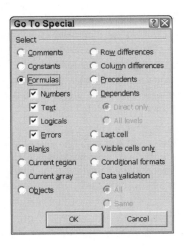

3. Select an option in the Go To Special dialog box.

4. Click OK.

Excel selects all cells that match your selected criterion.

To get an overall view of the worksheet structure if you're selecting special cells and to aid in tracking down potential errors, zooming out the worksheet to a small size is useful. **See** "Zooming Worksheets," in Part II, for more information on the Zoom feature.

Excel has some shortcut keys that you can use to select precedent and dependent cells without needing to use the Go To Special dialog box.

Key Combination	What It Selects
Ctrl+[	Direct precedents
Ctrl+Shift+[	All precedents
Ctrl+]	Direct dependents
Ctrl+Shift+]	All dependents

See also "Tracing Cell Relationships," later in this part.

Proofreading Your Worksheet Data

Excel provides a text-to-speech feature that you can use as an aid in proofreading your spreadsheet data. This tool is useful for the sight impaired but can also help if you're entering a lot of data manually — for example, from a printed sheet. While you're entering the data into a range, you can look at the printed sheet while Excel confirms each entry audibly. Or, if you've already entered the data, you can check the printed sheet while Excel speaks each entry.

To use the text-to-speech feature, you need to display the Text To Speech toolbar. Follow these steps to display the toolbar and use its options:

1. Choose Tools➪Speech➪Show Text To Speech Toolbar.

You can also choose View➪Toolbars➪Text To Speech.

Excel displays the Text To Speech toolbar.

2. If you want Excel to speak a range, select the range and click the By Rows or By Columns button to make Excel speak the cells across rows or down columns.

3. Click the Speak Cells button for Excel to start speaking the cells. Click the Stop Speaking button for Excel to stop speaking the cells.

4. If you want Excel to speak the cell every time that you enter data into a cell, click the Speak On Enter button. Click the button again to cancel the feature.

Remember: Your PC must have the appropriate equipment for the text-to-speech feature to work. At a minimum, you must have a sound card with speakers or a pair of headphones.

Remember: The Speak On Enter tool persists across Excel sessions — that is, if you enable it during one session and shut down Excel, it's still enabled the next time that you start Excel.

Spell Checking

Excel uses a spell checker that works just like the feature that you find in word-processing programs. You can access the spell checker by using any of the following methods:

🗸 Choose Tools⇨Spelling.

 🗸 Click the Spelling button on the Standard toolbar.

🗸 Press F7.

The extent of the spell checking depends on what you select after you access the dialog box.

What You Select	What Excel Checks
A single cell	The entire worksheet, including cell contents, notes, text in graphic objects and charts, and page headers and footers
A range of cells	Only that range
A group of characters	Only those characters in the Formula Bar

If Excel encounters a word that isn't in the current dictionary or is misspelled, it offers a list of suggestions that you can click to respond to.

Tracing Cell Relationships

Excel's auditing tools can help you track down errors in your worksheet by drawing arrows (known as *cell tracers*) to precedent and dependent cells. *Precedents* are cells that a formula refers to (either directly or indirectly). *Dependents* are formulas that depend on a particular cell.

Tracing precedents and dependents

To trace the precedents or dependents of a cell, follow these steps:

1. Click the cell that you want to trace.

2. Choose one of the following menu commands:

- Tools⇨Formula Auditing⇨Trace Precedents.

    You can also click the Trace Precedents button on the Formula Auditing toolbar.

    Excel draws arrows to all *direct* precedent cells.

- Tools⇨Formula Auditing⇨Trace Dependents.

    You can also click the Trace Dependents button on the Formula Auditing toolbar.

    Excel draws arrows to all *direct* dependent cells.

3. Repeat Step 2 as often as necessary to draw arrows to *indirect* precedent or *indirect* dependent cells.

4. Double-click an arrow to move the cell pointer to a precedent cell or dependent cell.

    If Excel displays a dashed line pointing to a miniature sheet icon, this indicator means that the precedent cells are on a different worksheet. Double-clicking the dashed line displays the Go To dialog box. Select a cell reference in the Go To dialog box, and click OK.

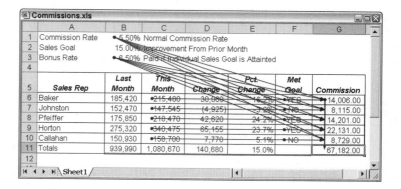

5. Choose Tools⇨Formula Auditing⇨Remove All Arrows after you finish tracing the source of your error.

    You can also click the Remove All Arrows button on the Formula Auditing toolbar.

This type of interactive tracing is often more revealing if you zoom out of the worksheet to display a larger area. *See* "Zooming Worksheets," in Part II.

See also "Tracing formula error values," immediately following in this part.

Tracing formula error values

Often, an error in one cell (for example, #DIV/0!, #VALUE!, #NA, and so on) is the result of an error in a precedent cell. Excel helps you to identify the cell or cells that are causing the error value to appear.

To trace the source of the error value, follow these steps:

1. Click the cell that contains the error.

2. Choose Tools⇔Formula Auditing⇔Trace Error.

You can also click the Trace Error button on the Formula Auditing toolbar.

Excel draws arrows to all *direct* precedent cells.

3. Repeat Step 2 as often as necessary to draw arrows to *indirect* precedent cells.

4. Double-click an arrow to move the cell pointer to a precedent cell.

5. Choose Tools⇔Formula Auditing⇔Remove All Arrows after you finish tracing the source of your error.

You can also click the Remove All Arrows button on the Formula Auditing toolbar.

See also "Formula Error Values" and "Tracing precedents and dependents," both earlier in this part.

Using the Watch Window

If you're attempting to track down certain problems with large spreadsheet models, the capability to display a window that shows the value of the formula cells if their associated precedents are in different parts of a worksheet, in different worksheets, or even in different open workbooks comes in handy. For example, this ability can be useful if you're unsure of the results that Excel is generating in certain formula cells after you change the values in precedent cells (that is, the cells that the formula refers to either directly or indirectly). This way, if you make changes to precedent cells, you can see the result of formulas immediately in the window. Excel provides the Watch Window to handle these situations.

Displaying and adding cells to the Watch Window

To display and add cells to the Watch Window, follow these steps:

1. Select the cells that you want to watch.

2. Choose Tools⇨Formula Auditing⇨Show Watch Window.

    You can also click the Show Watch Window button on the Formula Auditing toolbar.

   Excel displays the Watch Window.

3. Click Add Watch.

   Excel displays the Add Watch dialog box, with the cell references that you selected in Step 1 already filled in.

4. Click the Add button.

   Excel adds the cell references to the Watch Window.

5. To change the width of a column in the Watch Window, drag the boundary on the right side of the column heading.

6. To move the active cell pointer to the cell that an entry in the Watch Window refers to, double-click the entry.

7. To add cells from other worksheets or open workbooks, switch to the other worksheet or workbook and repeat Steps 1 through 4.

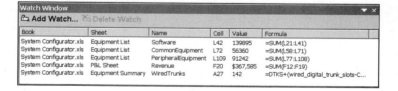

Book	Sheet	Name	Cell	Value	Formula
System Configurator.xls	Equipment List	Software	L42	139895	=SUM(L21:L41)
System Configurator.xls	Equipment List	CommonEquipment	L72	56360	=SUM(L58:L71)
System Configurator.xls	Equipment List	PeripheralEquipment	L109	91242	=SUM(L77:L108)
System Configurator.xls	P&L Sheet	Revenue	F20	$367,585	=SUM(F12:F19)
System Configurator.xls	Equipment Summary	WiredTrunks	A27	142	=DTKS+(wired_digital_trunk_slots-C...

Remember: Cells that contain links to other workbooks appear in the Watch Window only if the other workbooks are open.

 To select all the cells in a worksheet that contain formulas, in Step 1 choose Edit⇨Go To, click the Special button in the Go To dialog box that appears, select the Formulas option in the Go To Special dialog box that appears, and click OK.

Removing cells from the Watch Window

To remove cells from the Watch Window, follow these steps:

1. Select the cells in the Watch Window that you want to remove.

    To select multiple cells, press Ctrl and then click the cells.

2. Click Delete Watch.

Hiding the Watch Window

To hide the Watch Window from view, choose Tools⇨Formula
Auditing⇨Hide Watch Window or click the Show Watch Window
button on the Formula Auditing toolbar. (This button toggles the
Watch Window on and off.)

See also "Displaying and adding cells to the Watch Window," earlier
in this part.

Formatting Your Data

You have a lot of control over the appearance of information that you enter into a cell. Changing the appearance of cell contents is known as *formatting*. Formatting data in tables can make your worksheet more readable and presentable. In this part, you discover how to apply Excel's many formatting options.

In this part . . .

You can format cells before or after you enter information. If you're entering a series of numbers, for example, you can preformat the cells so that the numbers appear with commas and the desired number of decimal places.

Remember: Formatting doesn't affect the contents of your worksheet — only the way the text and values appear in the cell and in any succeeding printouts.

Adding Borders to a Cell or Range

People often use borders to "group" a range of similar cells or simply as a way to delineate rows or columns for aesthetic purposes.

To add borders around a cell or range, follow these steps:

1. Select the cell or range.

2. Choose Format⇨Cells from the menu bar (or press Ctrl+1).

   Excel displays the Format Cells dialog box.

3. Click the Border tab in the Format Cells dialog box.

4. Select a line style from the Style area of the dialog box.

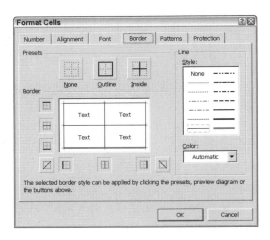

5. Select the border position for the line style by using any of or all the following combinations:

   • **Click one of the Presets buttons.** The three buttons (None, Outline, and Inside, respectively) enable you to quickly remove all borders, add a border around the outside of the selection, or add borders to the interior of the selection.

- **Click one of the Border buttons.** The Border buttons are *toggles* (that is, they either add or remove the border).

- **Click directly in the preview box.**

Excel displays the selected border style in the preview box. You can choose different styles for different border positions. You can also select a color for the border.

Notice that you can apply diagonal borders that extend through cells and ranges. Diagonal borders give the effect of the cells being "crossed out."

6. Click OK to apply the borders to your selection.

Excel enables you to draw borders directly on your worksheet. Follow these steps to apply borders by using the Borders toolbar.

1. Choose View⇨Toolbars⇨Borders to display the Borders toolbar.

2. Select a line style by clicking the Line Style drop-down list box and a line color by clicking the Line Color button.

3. Click the Draw Border button. The mouse pointer converts to a pencil icon.

The Draw Border button acts as a toggle. Clicking the button a second time deselects border drawing.

If you click the arrow on the Draw Border button, you see a second option, Draw Border Grid. Use this option to apply a border grid to a range.

4. Drag the mouse pointer around the cells to which you want to apply borders. Instead of dragging, you can also click the mouse pointer on the cell outlines to apply borders.

5. To erase a border, select the Erase Border button. The mouse pointer changes to an eraser icon. Drag or click the eraser over the cell or range borders that you want to erase. As does the Draw Border button, this button acts as a toggle.

 Another quick way to apply borders is to use the Borders tool on the Formatting toolbar. When you click the down arrow on the Borders button, Excel displays a palette from which you can select commonly used border styles.

Aligning Cell Contents

Excel's default alignments are such that cell contents appear at the bottom, numbers are right-aligned, text is left-aligned, and logical values are centered in cells. You can use Excel's alignment tools to change the default alignments that Excel applies to cell contents.

Setting horizontal and vertical alignment

You can use the following procedure to change the horizontal and vertical alignments of cell contents:

1. Select the cell or range of cells to align.

2. Choose Format⇔Cells from the menu bar (or press Ctrl+1).

   Excel displays the Format Cells dialog box.

3. Click the Alignment tab in the Format Cells dialog box.

4. Choose the desired horizontal or vertical alignment option from the appropriate drop-down lists.

5. Click OK.

See also "Indenting the contents of a cell," immediately following in this part.

You can apply the most common horizontal alignment options by selecting the cell or range of cells and using the following tools on the Formatting toolbar: Align Left, Center, and Align Right.

Indenting the contents of a cell

Excel enables you to indent text in a cell. Using this feature is much easier than padding the cell with spaces to indent. The following figure shows six cells that are indented.

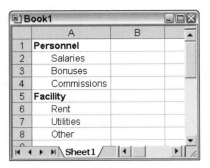

To indent the contents of a cell, follow these steps:

1. Select the cell or range of cells to indent.

2. Choose Format⇨Cells (or press Ctrl+1).

3. Click the Alignment tab in the Format Cells dialog box that appears.

4. Specify the number of spaces to indent in the Indent text box.

5. Click OK.

 The easiest way to change the indentation for selected cells is to use the Decrease Indent and Increase Indent tools on the Formatting toolbar.

Remember: Indented text is always left-aligned.

Justifying (refitting) text across cells

Justifying text redistributes the text in cells so that it fits into a specified range. You can make the text either wider (so that it uses fewer rows) or narrower (so that it uses more rows).

The following figure shows a range of text before and after redistribution to fit a specified range.

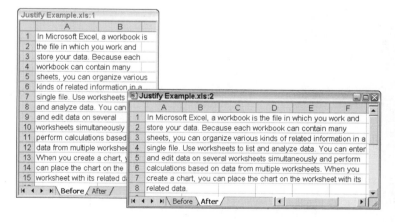

To justify text across cells, follow these steps:

1. Select the text that you want to justify.

   The text must lie in cells in a single column. Blank rows serve as paragraph markers.

2. Drag the mouse pointer to extend the selection to the right so that the selection is as wide as you want the end result to be.

3. Choose Edit⇨Fill⇨Justify.

Excel redistributes the text so that it fits within the selected range.

If the range you select isn't large enough to hold all the text, Excel warns you but permits you to continue or abort. Be careful: Justified text overwrites anything that gets in its way.

Remember: In all cases, the text must lie in a single column of cells. After you justify the text, it remains in a single column.

Wrapping text within a cell

Wrapping text within a cell is a good way to display more informa-tion without making the column wider. This technique is useful for lengthy table headings, as shown in the following figure.

	A	B	C	D	E	F
1						
2		Projected Sales ($000)	Actual Sales ($000)	Projected Minus Actual ($000)		
3	Computers	450	325	125		
4	Receivers	275	197	78		
5	Speakers	200	148	52		
6	DVD Players	150	245	-95		
7		1075	915	160		
8						

Equipment Sales.xls — Sheet1

To format a cell or range so that the words wrap, follow these steps:

1. Select the cell or range that you want to apply word wrap formatting to.

2. Choose Format⇨Cells (or press Ctrl+1).

3. Click the Alignment tab of the Format Cells dialog box that appears.

4. Select the Wrap Text check box.

5. Click OK to apply the formatting to the selection.

Remember: If you decrease the column width of a cell that you format with wrap text, the words wrap to the next line to accommo-date the new column width.

Applying Background Colors and Patterns

To change the background color or pattern that you use in cells, follow these steps:

1. Select the cell or range that you want to format.

2. Choose Format⇨Cells from the menu bar (or press Ctrl+1).

3. Click the Patterns tab in the Format Cells dialog box that appears.

4. Click a color on the Color grid.

5. To add a pattern, click the Pattern drop-down list box and select a pattern from the list.

   If you want, you can choose a second color for the pattern.

6. Click OK to apply the color and/or pattern.

Remember: If you use background colors or patterns, you may not receive the results that you want if you print with a noncolor printer.

See also "Printing Colors in Black and White," in Part VIII.

 A faster way to change the background color (but not a pattern) is to select the cells and then select a color from the Fill Color tool on the Formatting toolbar.

Applying a Background Graphic

In some cases, you may want to use a graphics file as a background for a worksheet — similar to the *wallpaper* that you may display on your Windows Desktop.

To add a background to a worksheet, follow these steps:

1. Activate the worksheet.

2. Choose Format⇨Sheet⇨Background from the menu bar.

   Excel displays the Sheet Background dialog box, which enables you to choose a graphics file.

3. Locate the graphics file that you want. (You may need to change to a different folder to locate the file.)

4. Click Insert, and Excel tiles your worksheet with the graphic that you selected in Step 3.

To get rid of a background graphic, choose Format⇨Sheet⇨ Delete Background from the menu bar.

Remember: The graphic background is for the screen display only; it doesn't show up on the page if you print the worksheet.

Changing the Appearance of Text in Cells

By default, Excel formats the information that you enter into a worksheet by using the 10-point Arial font. If you want various parts of your worksheet to stand out, however, such as the headers in a table, you can apply different font styles, sizes, colors, and attributes to the header cells.

Changing fonts and text sizes

The easiest way to change the font or text size for selected cells is to use the Font and Font Size tools on the Formatting toolbar. Just select the cells, click the appropriate tool, and select the font or size from the drop-down list.

You can also use the following technique, which enables you to control several other properties of the font from a single dialog box:

1. Select the cell or range to modify.

2. Choose Format⇨Cells (or press Ctrl+1).

3. Click the Font tab in the Format Cells dialog box that appears.

4. Make the desired changes, and click OK.

Notice that you also can change the font style (bold, italic), underlining, color, and effects (strikethrough, superscript, or subscript). If you select the Normal Font check box, Excel displays the selections for the font that it defines as the Normal style.

See also "Creating named styles," later in this part.

Applying colors to text

The following steps illustrate the fastest way to change the color of text:

1. Select the cell or range.

2. Select a color from the Font Color tool on the Formatting toolbar.

If you click the down-arrow button on the Font Color tool, the tool expands to show more colors.

Remember: You can also change text color in the Font tab of the Format Cells dialog box.

Changing text attributes

The easiest way to change common text attributes (bold, italic, and underline) is to select the cell or range and then click the appropriate tool on the Formatting toolbar (Bold, Italic, or Underline).

Or, you can use the following shortcut keys to modify the selected cells.

Format	Shortcut Keys
Bold	Ctrl+B
Italic	Ctrl+I
Underline	Ctrl+U
~~Strikethrough~~	Ctrl+5

These toolbar buttons and shortcut keys act as toggles. You can turn bold on and off, for example, by repeatedly pressing Ctrl+B (or clicking the Bold tool).

Changing Text Orientation (Direction)

Normally, the contents of a cell appear horizontally. In some cases, you may want to display the text vertically or even at an angle, as shown in the following figure.

	A	B	C	D	E	F
1						
2		2nd Qtr.	Unit-1	Unit-2	Unit-3	
3		January	132	232	546	
4		February	154	209	566	
5		March	165	312	433	
6						

Book4 — Sheet1

To change the orientation of text in a cell, follow these steps:

1. Select the cell or range to modify.

2. Choose Format⇨Cells (or press Ctrl+1).

3. Click the Alignment tab in the Format Cells dialog box.

4. In the Orientation area, adjust the text angle by dragging the orientation gauge or entering an angle (in degrees) in the

Degrees text box. You represent vertical text with an angle of 90 degrees (text rotating upward) or –90 degrees (text rotating downward).

5. Click OK to apply the new orientation to the selection.

To quickly rotate text 90 degrees downward, select the text and click the vertical box to the left of the orientation gauge.

Remember: Excel adjusts the row height to display the text. If you don't want this adjustment, you can use the Merge Cells feature to avoid a larger row height.

See also "Merging Cells," later in this part.

Copying Formats

The quickest way to copy the formats from one cell to another cell or range is to use the Format Painter button on the Standard toolbar. Follow these steps:

1. Select the cell or range with the formatting attributes that you want to copy.

2. Click the Format Painter button.

   Notice that the mouse pointer appears as a miniature paintbrush.

3. Select (paint) the cells to which you want to apply the formats.

4. Release the mouse button, and Excel copies the formats.

Double-clicking the Format Painter button causes the mouse pointer to remain a paintbrush after you release the mouse button. This paintbrush enables you to paint other areas of the worksheet with the same formats. To exit paint mode, click the Format Painter button again (or press Esc).

Follow these steps for another way to copy formats:

1. Select the cell or range that contains the formatting attributes that you want to copy.

2. Choose Edit➪Copy from the menu bar, or right-click the cell or range and choose Copy from the shortcut menu.

3. Select the cell or range to which you want to apply the formats.

4. Choose Edit➪Paste Special (or right-click the cell or range and choose Paste Special), click the Formats radio button in the Paste Special dialog box that appears, and click OK.

Formatting Based on a Cell's Contents

If you use conditional formatting, Excel automatically changes the formatting of a cell depending on the value in the cell. You may, for example, want to visually identify all cells in a range that exceed a certain value. You can specify up to three conditions for a cell by following these steps:

1. Select the cell or range that you want to format conditionally.

2. Choose Format⇨Conditional Formatting from the menu bar.

3. In the drop-down list box in the upper-left corner of the Conditional Formatting dialog box that appears, specify whether to base formatting on the cell's value (Cell Value Is) or the value of a formula in a different cell (Formula Is).

4. If you base the condition on the cell's value, specify in the remaining list/text boxes the condition (for example, Cell Value Is greater than 100). If you base the condition on a formula, enter the address that holds the formula in the text box. (The formula must evaluate to either True or False.)

5. Click the Format button, and in the Format Cells dialog box that appears, specify the formatting that you want to apply if the condition is true.

6. Choose your formatting options on the Font, Border, and Patterns tabs. Click OK after you finish to close the Format Cells dialog box.

7. To specify additional conditions for the selected cells, click the Add button and repeat Steps 3 through 5. (The dialog box expands, providing additional conditions.) You can specify up to three conditions.

   To delete one or more conditions for the selected cells, click the Delete button and click the check box(es) of the condition(s) you want to remove in the dialog box that appears. Click OK to complete the delete and remove the dialog box.

8. Click OK.

If the cell doesn't meet the condition (or conditions) that you specify, it takes on the standard formatting for the cell.

If you copy a cell containing conditional formatting, the conditional formatting applies to all copies.

Formatting Numbers

Excel internally stores all numbers and dates you enter in your worksheet as plain, unformatted numbers. You can use Excel's built-in numeric and date/time formats to make your data more readable and understandable. In addition, you can create a custom number format if you can't find a suitable built-in format to fit your needs.

Using Excel's built-in number formats

Excel is smart enough to perform some number formatting for you automatically. If you enter **9.6%** into a cell, for example, Excel knows that you want to use a percentage format and applies it for you automatically. Similarly, if you use commas to separate thousands (such as in **123,456**) or a dollar sign to indicate currency (such as in **$123.45**), Excel applies the appropriate formatting for you.

Use the Formatting toolbar to quickly apply common number formats. After you click one of these buttons, the active cell takes on the specified number format. The following table lists these toolbar buttons.

Button	Button Name	Formatting Applied
$	Currency Style	Adds a dollar sign to the left, separates thousands with a comma, and displays the value with two digits to the right of the decimal point
%	Percent Style	Displays the value as a percentage with no decimal places
,	Comma Style	Separates thousands with a comma and displays the value with two digits to the right of the decimal place
.0 .00	Increase Decimal	Increases the number of digits to the right of the decimal point by one
.00 .0	Decrease Decimal	Decreases the number of digits to the right of the decimal point by one

Remember: These five toolbar buttons actually apply predefined *styles* to the selected cells, which isn't the same as simply changing the number format.

If none of the predefined number formats fit the bill, you need to use the Format Cells dialog box; to do so, follow these steps:

1. Select the cell or range that contains the values to format.

2. Choose Format⇨Cells (or press Ctrl+1).

3. Click the Number tab on the Format Cells dialog box that appears.

4. Select one of the 12 categories of number formats.

   After you select a category from the list box, the right side of the dialog box changes to display appropriate options.

5. Select an option from the right side of the dialog box.

   Options vary, depending on your category choice. The top of the dialog box displays a sample of how the active cell appears with the selected number format.

6. After you make your choices, click OK to apply the number format to all the selected cells.

Remember: If the cell displays a series of pound signs (such as ######), it means that the column isn't wide enough to display the value using the number format that you selected. The solution is to make the column wider or to change the number format. *See* "Changing column width," later in this part.

Creating custom number formats

Excel provides you with quite a few predefined number formats. If none of these formats are satisfactory, you need to create a custom number format. Just follow these steps:

1. Select the cell or range of cells that contains the values that you want to format.

2. Choose Format⇨Cells from the menu bar (or press Ctrl+1).

3. Click the Number tab in the Format Cells dialog box that appears.

4. Click the Custom category option at the bottom of the Category list box.

5. Construct a number format by specifying a series of codes in the Type text box.

6. Click OK to store the custom number format and apply it to the selected cells.

   The custom number format is now available for you to use with other cells.

Excel's online Help describes the formatting codes that are available for custom number formats, date, and time. To see some examples of formatting codes, click the Custom category option in the Number tab of the Format Cells dialog box.

Remember: Excel stores custom number formats with the workbook. To make the custom format available in a different workbook, you must copy a cell that uses the custom format to the other workbook.

Formatting a Table Automatically

The Excel AutoFormat feature applies attractive formatting to a table automatically.

To use AutoFormat, follow these steps:

1. Move the cell pointer anywhere within a table that you want to format. (Excel determines the table's boundaries automatically.)

2. Choose Format⇨AutoFormat.

   Excel responds by opening its AutoFormat dialog box.

3. Select one of the 17 AutoFormats from the list, and click OK.

   Excel formats the table using the selected AutoFormat.

   If you attempt to apply an AutoFormat in a cell where all the surrounding cells are blank, Excel displays an error message.

You can't define your own AutoFormats, but you *can* control the type of formatting that Excel applies. If you click the Options button in the AutoFormat dialog box, the dialog box expands to show six options.

Initially, the six check boxes are all selected, which means that Excel applies formatting from all six categories. To skip one or more categories, just deselect the appropriate check boxes by clicking them before you click OK.

Hiding Cell Contents

You can "hide" the contents of a cell by using either of the following formatting options:

✔ Apply a custom number format consisting of three semicolons (; ; ;).

✔ Make the text color the same as the background color.

Both formatting techniques have the same flaw: If the cell pointer is on the cell, its contents are visible in the Formula Bar. To avoid this flaw and make the cell contents truly invisible, follow these steps:

1. Select the cell or range and make the text color the same as the background color, or apply a custom number format consisting

of three semicolons (; ; ;). (*See* "Applying colors to text" and "Creating custom number formats," both earlier in this part, for details.)

2. Choose Format⇨Cells (or press Ctrl+1).

   Excel displays the Format Cells dialog box.

3. Click the Protection tab.

4. Select the Hidden check box.

5. Click OK.

6. Choose Tools⇨Protection⇨Protect Sheet to turn on the Hidden attribute for the selected cells.

See also "Protecting a Worksheet," in Part II.

Hiding and Unhiding Columns and Rows

Hiding columns and rows is useful if you don't want users to see particular information or if you don't want some information to print. Alternatively, you can unhide rows or columns to reveal information.

Hiding columns and rows

To hide a column(s) or row(s), follow these steps:

1. Select the column(s) or row(s) that you want to hide. (*See* "Selecting entire rows and columns," in Part III, for details.)

2. Choose Format⇨Column⇨Hide or Format⇨Row⇨Hide from the menu bar, or right-click the column or row and select Hide from the shortcut menu.

You also can drag a column's right border to the left or a row's bottom border upward to hide it.

Remember: A hidden column or row has a width or height of 0. If you use the arrow keys to move the cell pointer, you skip cells in hidden columns or rows. In other words, you can't use the arrow keys to move to a cell in a hidden row or column.

See also "Unhiding columns and rows," immediately following in this part.

Unhiding columns and rows

Unhiding a hidden row or column can prove a bit tricky because you can't directly select a row or column that's hidden. To unhide a hidden column or row, follow these steps:

1. Select the rows or columns on either side of the hidden rows or columns. (**See** "Selecting entire rows and columns," in Part III, for details.)

   If columns G and H are hidden, for example, select columns F and I.

	C	D	E	F		J	K	
		Last	This					
5	Sales Rep	Month	Month	Change	Commission			
6	Baker	185,420	215,480	30,060	14,006.00			
7	Johnston	152,470	147,545	(4,925)	8,115.00			
8	Pfeiffer	175,850	218,470	42,620	14,201.00			
9	Horton	275,320	340,475	65,155	22,131.00			
10	Callahan	150,930	158,700	7,770	8,729.00			
11	Totals	939,990	1,080,670	140,680	67,182.00			

Commissions.xls — Sheet1

2. Choose Format➪Row➪Unhide or Format➪Column➪Unhide from the menu bar, or right-click anywhere in the selection and choose Unhide from the shortcut menu.

To unhide all hidden columns or rows, select the entire worksheet (by pressing Ctrl+A or clicking the blank box that intersects the row and column headings) and then choose Format➪Row➪Unhide or Format➪Column➪Unhide.

See also "Selecting entire rows and columns," in Part III, and "Hiding columns and rows," immediately preceding in this part.

Merging Cells

Excel offers a helpful feature that enables you to merge cells into a single, larger cell. This feature enables you to have cells of unequal sizes. If you have a table that spans six columns, for example, you can merge six cells at the top to form a single larger cell for the table's title. In the following figure, cells D2:F2 are merged horizontally, and cells B4:B7 are merged vertically.

You should be aware of the following things when merging cells:

✔ You can merge cells horizontally or vertically.

✔ If a selection contains more than one nonempty cell, the merged cells contain the contents and formatting of the upper-left cell of the merged range.

✔ Understanding that *cells* get merged — not the *contents* of cells — is very important. Whenever you merge cells, you receive a warning if the selected range contains more than one nonempty cell.

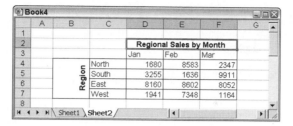

To merge a range of cells, follow these steps:

1. Select the cells that you want to merge.

2. Choose Format⇨Cells (or press Ctrl+1).

    Excel displays the Format Cells dialog box.

3. Click the Alignment tab.

4. Select the Merge Cells check box.

5. Click OK.

To unmerge cells, select the cells and deselect the Merge cells check box on the Alignment tab of the Format Cells dialog box.

 You can merge cells and center cell contents by using the Merge and Center button on the Formatting toolbar. To unmerge the cells, click the Merge and Center button again.

Modifying Cell Size

You may want to change the width of a column if it's not wide enough to display values (displaying a series of pound signs — ########) or to simply to space out the cells horizontally. Changing the row height is useful for spacing out rows — changing the row height is better than inserting empty rows between rows of data.

Changing column width

Before changing the width of a column, you can select a number of columns so that the selected columns all have the same width.

Use any of the following methods to change the width of selected columns.

✔ Choose Format⇨Column⇨Width, and enter a value in the Column width text box in the Column Width dialog box that appears.

✔ Drag the right border of the column heading with the mouse until the column is the width that you want.

■ Book4			Width: 10.33 (100 pixels)	□ ×
	A	B	C	D	E
1			######		
2			######		
3			######		
4			######		
5					

H ◄ ► H \ Sheet1 / Sheet2 \ Sheet3 /

 ✔ Choose Format⇨Column⇨AutoFit Selection. This command adjusts the width of the selected column(s) so that the widest entry in the column fits.

 ✔ Double-click the right border of a column heading to automatically set the column width to the widest entry in the column.

To change the default width of all columns, select Format⇨Column⇨ Standard Width. This command opens the Standard Width dialog box, in which you enter the new default column width. All columns that weren't previously adjusted take on the new column width.

Changing row height

You measure row height in *points* (a standard unit of measurement in the printing trade; 72 points equal 1 inch). If you want, you can select several rows before using the following techniques to set row height:

 ✔ Drag the lower row border with the mouse until the row is the height that you want.

 ✔ Choose Format⇨Row⇨Height, and enter a value (in points) in the Row Height text box in the Row Height dialog box that appears.

 ✔ Double-click the bottom border of a row to automatically set the row height to the tallest entry in the row. You also can select Format⇨Row⇨AutoFit for this task.

Remember: The default row height depends on the font that you define in the Normal style. Excel adjusts row heights automatically to accommodate the tallest font in the row. So if you change the font size of a cell to, say, 20 points, Excel makes the row taller so that the entire text is visible.

Using Named Styles

If you find yourself continuously applying the same combination of fonts, lines, shading, number format, and so on in your worksheet, creating and using named styles is to your advantage. A *named style* can consist of settings for six different attributes. A style doesn't, however, need to use *all* the attributes. The attributes that can make up a style are as follows:

- ✔ Number format
- ✔ Font (type, size, and color)
- ✔ Alignment (vertical and horizontal)
- ✔ Borders
- ✔ Pattern
- ✔ Protection (locked and hidden)

Creating named styles

The easiest way to create a style is "by example," which means that you format a cell to have the style characteristics that you want and then have Excel create the style from that cell. To create a style by example, follow these steps:

1. Select a cell, and apply the formatting that you want to make up the style.

2. Choose Format⇨Style.

   Excel displays its Style dialog box.

3. Enter a name for the style in the Style Name drop-down list box.

4. Deselect the check boxes for any of the six attributes that you *don't* want to be part of the style (optional).

5. Click OK to create the style.

The new style is available, and you can apply it to other cells or ranges.

See also "Applying named styles," "Changing the Appearance of Text in Cells," "Formatting Numbers," and other cell-formatting options, elsewhere in this part.

Applying named styles

Excel enables you to associate a named style with any cell. By default, all cells have the Normal style. In addition, Excel provides five other built-in styles — all of which control only the cell's number format. We list the styles available in every workbook in the following table.

Style Name	Description	Number Format
Normal	Excel's default style	1234
Comma*	Comma with two decimal places	1,234.00
Comma[0]	Comma with no decimal places	1,234
Currency*	Left-aligned dollar sign with comma and two decimal places	$1,234.00
Currency[0]	Left-aligned dollar sign with comma and no decimal places	$1,234
Percent*	Percent with no decimal places	12%

*You can apply this style by clicking a button on the Standard toolbar.

Excel also enables you to create your own styles (for both numbers and text). To apply a custom style or a style that isn't associated with a toolbar button, follow these steps:

1. Select the cell or range to which you want to apply the style.

2. Choose Format⇨Style from the menu bar.

   Excel displays its Style dialog box.

3. Select the style from the Style Name drop-down list box.

   This list displays the Excel built-in styles and your own styles (if any).

4. Click OK to apply the style to the selection.

See also "Creating named styles," immediately preceding in this part.

Part VIII

Printing Your Work

Many worksheets that you develop with Excel are designed to serve as printed reports. Printing from Excel is quite easy, and you can generate attractive reports with minimal effort. Excel offers numerous printing options, however, which we explain in this part.

In this part . . .

Clicking the Print button on the Standard toolbar is a quick way to print the current worksheet by using the default settings. If you changed any of the default print settings, Excel uses the settings that you entered; otherwise, it uses the following default settings:

- ✔ Prints the active worksheet (or all selected worksheets), including any embedded charts or drawing objects.

- ✔ Prints one copy.

- ✔ Prints the entire worksheet. (By default, Excel prints all active worksheets.)

- ✔ Prints in portrait mode.

- ✔ Does not scale the printed output.

- ✔ Uses 1-inch margins for the top and bottom and ¾-inch margins for the left and right.

- ✔ Does not print a header or footer.

- ✔ For wide worksheets that span multiple pages, prints down and then over.

Adjusting Margins

Margins are the blank spaces that border a printed page (top, bottom, left, and right). The wider the margins, the less space that is available for printing. You can control all four page margins from within Excel.

To adjust the margins, follow these steps:

1. Choose File➪Page Setup from the menu bar.

2. Click the Margins tab in the Page Setup dialog box that appears.

3. Click the appropriate spinner to change the margin value (or enter a value directly in one of the text boxes).

4. Click OK to close the Page Setup dialog box.

In addition to changing the page margins, you can adjust the distance of the header from the top of the page and the distance of the footer from the bottom of the page. These settings should be less than the corresponding margin; otherwise, the header or footer may overlap the printed output. ***See also*** "Changing the Header or Footer," later in this part.

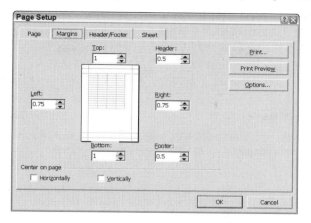

You also can change the margins while you're previewing your output — this is ideal for last-minute adjustments before printing.

See also "Previewing Your Work," later in this part.

Remember: The sample "page preview" picture in the Margins tab of the Page Setup dialog box is a bit deceiving because it doesn't really show you how your changes look in relation to the page. Instead, it simply displays a darker line to show you which margins you're adjusting.

Centering Printed Output

Normally, Excel prints a page at the top and left margins. If you want the output to be centered vertically or horizontally on the page, follow these steps:

1. Choose File➪Page Setup.

2. Click the Margins tab of the Page Setup dialog box that appears.

3. Select the appropriate check boxes in the Center on Page area: Horizontally or Vertically.

4. Click OK to close the Page Setup dialog box.

Changing Default Print Settings by Using a Template

If you find that you're never satisfied with the Excel default print settings, you may want to create a template with the print settings that you use most often. To create such a template, follow these steps:

1. Start with an empty workbook. (*See* "The Basics: Creating an Empty Workbook File," in The Big Picture part, for details.)

2. Adjust the print settings to your liking. (Use the appropriate section in this part if you need assistance with a particular setting.)

3. Save the workbook as a template in your xlstart folder, using the name **Book.xlt**. (*See* "Creating a default workbook template," in Part I, for details.)

Excel uses this template as the basis for all new workbooks, and your custom print settings become the default settings.

Changing the Header or Footer

A *header* is information that appears at the top of each printed page. A *footer* is information that appears at the bottom of each printed page.

Headers and footers each have three sections: left, center, and right. You can, for example, specify a header that consists of your name left-justified, the worksheet name centered, and the page number right-justified.

Remember: In Excel, the default is to have no header or footer.

Selecting a predefined header or footer

To select a predefined header or footer, follow these steps:

1. Choose File➪Page Setup from the menu bar.

2. Click the Header/Footer tab of the Page Setup dialog box that appears.

3. Select a header and/or footer from the Header or Footer drop-down list.

4. Click OK to close the Page Setup dialog box.

Creating a custom header or footer

To define a custom header or footer, follow these steps:

1. Choose File➪Page Setup.

2. Click the Header/Footer tab of the Page Setup dialog box that appears.

3. Click the Custom Header or Custom Footer button.

   Excel displays the Header or Footer dialog box, as appropriate.

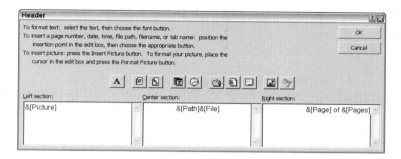

4. Enter the desired information in any of or all the three sections. Or click any of the nine buttons (which I describe in the following table) to enter a special code.

5. Click OK to close the Header (or Footer) dialog box, and then click OK to close the Page Setup dialog box.

Button	Description	Code	Function
A	Font	Not applicable	Enables you to choose a font for the selected text
	Page Number	&[Page]	Inserts the page number
	Total Pages	&[Pages]	Inserts the total number of pages to print
	Date	&[Date]	Inserts the current date
	Time	&[Time]	Inserts the current time
	File Path	&[Path]&[File]	Inserts the path and filename of the workbook
	File Name	&[File]	Inserts the workbook's name
	Sheet Name	&[Tab]	Inserts the sheet's name
	Insert Picture	&[Picture]	Enables you to choose a picture to insert in the header or footer

The Format Picture button on the Header/Footer toolbar is available only if you insert a picture in the header or footer. Clicking this button displays the Format Picture dialog box, in which you can select options to size, rotate, scale, crop, and adjust the picture.

 You can combine text and codes and insert as many codes as you want into each section. If the text that you enter uses an ampersand (&), you must enter it twice (because Excel uses an ampersand to signal a code). For example, to enter the text *Research & Development* into a section of a header or footer, type **Research && Development**.

 You can use as many lines as you want. Press Enter to force a line break for multiline headers or footers.

Controlling Page Settings

Excel provides several options that enable you to control how a page prints — orientation, paper size, scaling, and so on. This section describes how to use the Page Setup dialog box to set the more common page options.

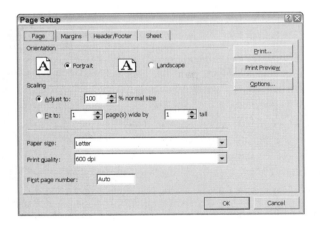

Changing page orientation

To change the page orientation (to landscape or portrait) of your printed output, follow these steps:

1. Choose File➪Page Setup from the menu bar.

2. Click the Page tab of the Page Setup dialog box that appears.

3. Select either the Portrait (tall pages) or Landscape (wide pages) radio button. Portrait is the default option.

4. Click OK to close the Page Setup dialog box.

Use landscape orientation if you have a wide range that doesn't fit on a vertically oriented page.

Selecting paper size

To change the paper size of the printed output, follow these steps:

1. Choose File⇨Page Setup.

2. Click the Page tab of the Page Setup dialog box.

3. Select the paper size from the Paper Size drop-down list.

4. Click OK to close the Page Setup dialog box.

Scaling your printed output

To scale your printed output, follow these steps:

1. Choose File⇨Page Setup.

2. Click the Page tab of the Page Setup dialog box.

3. Click the Adjust to radio button (if it is not already selected) and manually enter a scaling factor in the % Normal Size text box, or have Excel scale the output automatically to fit on the desired number of pages by clicking the Fit To radio button and entering the page information in the corresponding text boxes.

   To return to normal scaling, click the Adjust to radio button (if it is not already selected) and enter **100** in the % Normal Size text box.

4. Click OK to close the Page Setup dialog box.

Specifying the beginning page number

If you intend to insert your printed output into another report, you may want to specify a beginning page number so that the pages collate correctly as you insert them into the report. To do so, follow these steps:

1. Choose File⇨Page Setup.

2. Click the Page tab of the Page Setup dialog box.

3. Specify a page number for the first page in the First Page Number text box. The default option is set to Auto, which starts numbering at page 1.

4. Click OK to close the Page Setup dialog box.

Dealing with Page Breaks

If you print multiple-page reports, you know that controlling the page breaks is often important. You normally don't want a row to print on a page by itself, for example.

Excel handles page breaks automatically. After you print or preview your worksheet, Excel displays dashed lines to indicate where page breaks occur. Sometimes, you want to force a page break — either a vertical or a horizontal one. If your worksheet consists of several distinct areas, for example, you may want to print each area on a separate sheet of paper.

Inserting manual page breaks

To override Excel's automatic handling of page breaks, you must manually insert one or more page breaks. To insert a horizontal page break, follow these steps:

1. Move the cell pointer to the row that you want to begin the new page, but make sure that the cell pointer is in column A. (Otherwise, you insert a vertical page break *and* a horizontal page break.)

2. Choose Insert⇨Page Break from the menu bar to create the page break.

   Excel inserts the page break in the row that is above the cell pointer.

To insert a vertical page break, follow these steps:

1. Move the cell pointer to the column that you want to begin the new page, but make sure that the cell pointer is in row 1. (Otherwise, you insert a horizontal page break *and* a vertical page break).

2. Choose Insert⇨Page Break to create the page break.

   Excel inserts the page break in the column to the left of the cell pointer.

 When manipulating page breaks, using the Zoom feature to zoom out in the worksheet is often helpful. Doing so gives you a bird's-eye view of the worksheet, and you can see more pages at once. *See also* "Zooming Worksheets," in Part II.

Removing manual page breaks

To remove a manual page break, follow these steps:

1. Move the cell pointer anywhere in the first row beneath a
horizontal page break or in the first column to the right of a
vertical page break.

2. Choose Insert⇨Remove Page Break.

To remove all manual page breaks in the worksheet, click the Select
All button (or press Ctrl+A); then choose Insert⇨Reset All Page
Breaks. (The Select All button is the unlabeled box in the upper-left
corner of the spreadsheet, where the row numbers and column letters intersect.)

Previewing and adjusting page breaks

Excel offers a Page Break Preview viewing mode. The View⇨Page
Break Preview menu command displays your worksheet in a way
that enables you to move the page breaks by dragging them with
your mouse. This view doesn't show a true page preview. (It doesn't,
for example, show headers and footers.) But it's an easy way to make
sure that the pages break at desired locations.

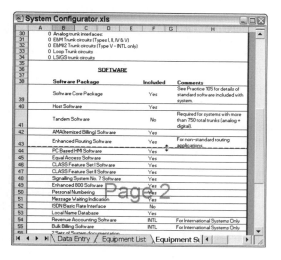

Remember the following points as you use the Page Break Preview
mode:

✔ Excel automatically zooms out so that you can see more on-
screen. You can set the zoom factor to any value that you want.

✔ If you specify a print area (rather than the entire worksheet), the print area appears in white and all the other cells appear in a darker color.

✔ You can change a page break by dragging it.

✔ While you're previewing the page breaks, you have full access to all of Excel's commands. To return to normal viewing, select View⇨Normal.

Remember: If you increase the amount of information to be printed on a page, Excel automatically scales the output to fit.

Previewing Your Work

The Excel Print Preview feature shows an image of the printed output on your screen — a handy feature that saves time and paper.

You can access the Print Preview feature in several ways, as the following list describes:

✔ Choose File⇨Print Preview from the menu bar.

 ✔ Click the Print Preview button on the Standard toolbar. You can also press and hold Shift and click the Print button on the Standard toolbar. (The Print button serves a dual purpose.)

✔ Choose File⇨Print, and click the Preview button in the Print dialog box.

✔ Choose File⇨Page Setup, and click the Print Preview button in the Page Setup dialog box.

Any of these methods changes the Excel window to the Print Preview window. The Print Preview window has several buttons along the top, and the most important is Margins. Clicking this button displays adjustable column and margin markers. You can drag the column or margin markers to make changes that appear on-screen. Click the Close button to exit Print Preview mode.

Printing Cell Comments

If one or more cells in your worksheet have a cell comment, you can print these comments along with the worksheet by following these steps:

1. Choose File⇨Page Setup from the menu bar.

2. Click the Sheet tab in the Page Setup dialog box that appears.

3. From the Comments drop-down list box, choose one of the following items:

- **(None):** Comments don't print. This option is the default.

- **At end of sheet:** All comments print at the end of the printout, beginning on a new sheet.

- **As displayed on sheet:** Comments print exactly where and as they appear. Only visible comments print.

4. Click OK to close the Page Setup dialog box.

Printing Charts

Nothing is particularly special about printing embedded charts; the process works just like that of printing a worksheet. As long as you include the embedded chart in the range to print, the chart prints as it appears on-screen.

Remember: If you print in Draft mode, embedded charts don't print.

If you don't want a particular embedded chart to appear on your printout, just follow these steps:

1. Right-click the chart.

2. Choose Format Chart Area from the shortcut menu that appears.

3. Click the Properties tab in the Format Object dialog box that appears.

4. Deselect the Print Object check box.

5. Click OK to close the dialog box.

If the chart is on a *chart sheet* (a special sheet that can hold a single chart but no data), the chart prints on a page by itself. If you access the Excel Page Setup dialog box while the chart sheet is active, you find that a Chart tab replaces the Sheet tab.

The Chart tab has several options, as the following list describes:

- ✓ **Use Full Page:** The chart prints to the full width and height of the page margins. Use Full Page usually isn't a good choice because the chart's relative proportions change, and you lose the WYSIWYG (what-you-see-is-what-you-get) advantage.

- ✓ **Scale to Fit Page:** This option expands the chart proportionally in both dimensions until one dimension fills the space between the margins. This option usually results in the best printout.

✔ **Custom:** This option prints the chart as it appears on-screen. Select View⇨Sized with Window to make the chart correspond to the window size and proportions. The chart prints at the current window size and proportions.

 Choosing the Print in Black and White option prints the data series with black-and-white patterns rather than colors. This option is useful if you don't have a color printer.

Printing Colors in Black and White

If you have a colorful worksheet but your printer is stuck in a monochrome world, you may discover that the worksheet colors don't translate well to black and white. In this case, you need to instruct Excel to ignore the colors while printing; to do so, follow these steps:

1. Choose File⇨Page Setup from the menu bar.

2. Click the Sheet tab of the Page Setup dialog box that appears.

3. Select the Black and White check box.

4. Click OK to close the Page Setup dialog box.

Printing in Draft Quality

Printing in Draft mode doesn't print embedded charts or drawing objects, cell gridlines, or borders. This mode usually reduces the printing time and is handy for getting a quick printout.

To print your work in Draft mode, follow these steps:

1. Choose File⇨Page Setup.

2. Click the Sheet tab of the Page Setup dialog box.

3. Select the Draft Quality check box.

4. Click OK to close the Page Setup dialog box.

Printing or Substituting Error Values

Excel gives you the option to print error values as they appear on your worksheet or to replace each of the error values with a predefined character in the printed output. Error values include #NUM!, #DIV/0!, #REF!, #N/A, #VALUE!, #NAME?, and #NULL!.

To select how error values appear in your printed output, follow these steps:

1. Choose File⇨Page Setup from the menu bar.

2. Click the Sheet tab of the Page Setup dialog box that appears.

3. Choose an option from the Cell Errors As drop-down list box.

4. Click OK to close the Page Setup dialog box.

Printing or Suppressing Gridlines

To change the way Excel handles worksheet gridlines when printing, follow these steps:

1. Choose File⇨Page Setup.

2. Click the Sheet tab of the Page Setup dialog box.

3. Select the Gridlines check box to print gridlines; deselect the check box to suppress gridline printing.

4. Click OK to close the Page Setup dialog box.

Printing Row and Column Headings

To make it easy to identify specific cell addresses from a printout, you want to print the row and column headings. To do so, follow these steps:

1. Choose File⇨Page Setup.

2. Click the Sheet tab of the Page Setup dialog box.

3. Select the Row and Column Headings check box.

4. Click OK to close the Page Setup dialog box.

Selecting Global Print Options

The following sections discuss the options that are available in the Print dialog box. The Print dialog box is where you actually start the printing (unless you use the Print button on the Standard toolbar). After you select your print settings, click OK in the Print dialog box to print your work.

Printing noncontiguous ranges

Excel enables you to specify a print area that consists of noncontiguous ranges (a multiple selection). To do so, follow these steps:

1. Press and hold Ctrl as you select the ranges.

2. Choose File⇨Print from the menu bar to open the Print dialog box.

3. Select the Selection option, and click OK.

This feature is handy, but you may not like the fact that Excel prints each range on a new sheet of paper.

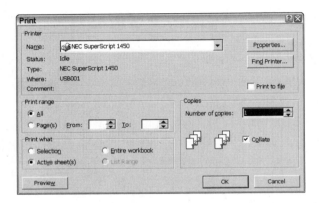

Printing selected pages

If your printed output uses multiple pages, you may not always want to print all the pages. To select a range of pages to print, follow these steps:

1. Choose File⇨Print from the menu bar.

2. In the Print range section of the Print dialog box that appears, indicate the number of the first and last pages to print. You can use the spinner controls, or you can type the page numbers in the text boxes.

Remember: Excel enables you to select only a contiguous range of pages to print.

Selecting a printer

If you have access to more than one printer, you may need to select the correct printer before printing. To do so, follow these steps:

1. Choose File⇨Print to open the Print dialog box.

2. In the Print dialog box, select the printer from the Name drop-down list box.

The Print dialog box also lists information about the selected printer, such as its status and where it connects.

Setting the print area

To specify a particular range to print, follow these steps:

1. Select the range that you want to print. Press and hold Ctrl to select nonadjacent ranges.

2. Choose File⇨Print Area⇨Set Print Area.

You can use the following steps to print only a specific range:

1. Select a range of cells.

2. Choose File⇨Print.

3. Choose the Selection option in the Print dialog box.

Specifying the data range to print

Excel gives you several options to determine the range of data in your worksheet or workbook that it prints. To tell Excel what data to print, follow these steps:

1. Choose File⇨Print.

2. In the Print What area of the Print dialog box, specify what to print. You have the following three options:

- **Selection:** Prints only the range that you select before choosing File⇨Print.

- **Active Sheet(s):** Prints the active sheet or all sheets that you select. You can select multiple sheets by pressing and holding Ctrl and clicking the sheet tabs. If you select multiple sheets, each sheet begins printing on a new page. This option is Excel's default print mode.

- **Entire Workbook:** Prints the entire workbook, including chart sheets, dialog sheets, and VBA modules.

Remember: If you choose the Active Sheet(s) option, Excel prints the entire sheet — or just the range named Print_Area. Each worksheet can have a range named Print_Area. You can set the print area (and Excel automatically creates the Print_Area name) by selecting it and then choosing File⇨Print Area⇨Set Print Area. Print_Area is a standard named range, so you can edit the range's reference manually if you like.

See also "Redefining Name References," in Part V.

Setting Print Titles

Many worksheets are set up with titles in the first row and descriptive names in the first column. If such a worksheet requires more than one page to print, you may find reading subsequent pages difficult because the text in the first row and first column doesn't print on subsequent pages. Excel offers a simple solution: *print titles*.

To specify print titles, follow these steps:

1. Choose File⇨Page Setup from the menu bar.

2. Click the Sheet tab of the Page Setup dialog box that appears.

3. Click inside the appropriate box in the Print Titles area, and point to the rows or columns in the worksheet.

   You can also enter these references manually. For example, to specify rows 1 and 2 as repeating rows, enter **1:2**.

4. Click OK to close the Page Setup dialog box.

Remember: Don't confuse print titles with headers; these are two different concepts. Headers appear at the top of each page and contain information such as the worksheet name, date, or page number. Print titles describe the data that you're printing, such as field names in a database table or list.

 You can specify different print titles for each worksheet in the workbook. Excel remembers print titles by creating sheet-level names (Print_Titles).

Specifying Page Order

If you have a worksheet that spans across several columns and down several rows, your worksheet is likely to end up with multiple vertical and/or horizontal page breaks. In this case, you have the choice of printing your worksheet pages from left to right or from top to bottom.

To set the page order for printed pages, follow these steps:

1. Choose File⇨Page Setup.

2. Click the Sheet tab of the Page Setup dialog box.

3. In the Page Order area, click the Down, Then Over radio button or the Over, Then Down radio button.

   Excel displays a sample picture to the right of the options, which shows the direction in which the document is to print.

4. Click OK to close the Page Setup dialog box.

Part IX

Charting Your Data

A chart is a way to present a table of numbers visually. Excel provides you with the tools to create a wide variety of highly customizable charts. In this part, we show you how to use the important chart-making options in Excel.

In this part . . .

When you create a chart, you can embed the chart on the worksheet containing the data from which you create the chart, or you can use a separate chart sheet. A chart sheet contains a single chart (which occupies the entire sheet) that is linked to the data in a worksheet.

Before you can do anything with a chart, you must activate it, as follows:

✔ To activate a chart on a chart sheet, click the chart sheet's tab.

✔ To activate a chart that you embed in a worksheet, click the chart border area.

If you click an embedded chart, you're actually selecting the part that you're clicking.

Adding Elements to a Chart

After you create a chart, you may decide that you want to add additional information on the chart, such as a new data series, a trend-line, or error bars. The following sections explain how to add these elements to an existing chart.

Adding a new data series to a chart

You can add a new data series to a chart in several ways, as the following list describes:

✔ Select the range that you want to add, and drag it into the chart. After you release the mouse button, Excel updates the chart with the data that you drag into it. This technique works only if the chart is embedded in the worksheet.

✔ Activate the chart, and choose Chart⇨Add Data. Excel displays a dialog box that prompts you for the range of data to add to the chart. Enter the range manually, or select the range in the worksheet by using the mouse pointer.

✔ Select the range that you want to add, and copy it to the Windows Clipboard. Then activate the chart, and choose Edit⇨Paste Special. Excel responds by opening the Paste Special dialog box. Complete the information in this dialog box to correspond to the data that you selected.

✔ Activate the chart, and then click the Chart Wizard tool. You see the first Chart Wizard dialog box. Click the Next button to get to the second dialog box. Edit the range reference to include the new data series (or point to the new range in the worksheet). Click Finish, and Excel updates the chart with the new data.

Adding a trendline to a data series

If you're plotting data over time, you may want to plot a *trendline,* which points out general trends in your data. In some cases, you also can forecast future data by using trendlines.

To add a trendline to a data series, follow these steps:

1. Activate the chart, as we describe at the beginning of this part.

2. Click one of the data points in the series. This action selects the entire data series.

    Be careful not to click a data point after you select the entire series, because this action selects only a single data point. If you accidentally select a single data point, click anywhere outside the data series and repeat the step.

3. Choose Chart⇨Add Trendline from the menu bar, or right-click a data point and choose Add Trendline from the shortcut menu that appears.

4. Click the Type tab of the Add Trendline dialog box that appears, and select the type of trendline that you want; then click OK.

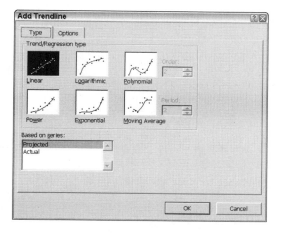

 You can also set options by clicking the Options tab of the Add Trendline dialog box. The Options tab enables you to specify a name to appear in the legend and the number of periods that you want to forecast. Two additional options enable you to specify that the equation that Excel uses for the trendline and the R^2 value appear on the chart.

Remember: After Excel inserts a trendline, the trendline may look like a new data series, but it's not. The trendline is a new chart element with a name, such as *Series 1 Trendline 1*. You can double-click a trendline to change its formatting or its options. A series can have more than one trendline.

Remember: You can't add trendlines to all chart types. If the Chart⇨Add Trendline command isn't accessible (for example, the command is grayed out), you can't add a trendline to the series that you chose.

Adding Fill Effects to a Chart

You can modify the fill pattern that you use in various chart elements to produce dramatic or unusual effects. You can modify the fill pattern for the chart area, the plot area, columns, and bars.

To add fill effects to a chart element's fill pattern, follow these steps:

1. Double-click the chart element that you want to modify.

   Excel displays a dialog box that is appropriate to the element that you select.

2. Select the Patterns tab. (This tab is the default, however, so it may already be selected as the dialog box opens.)

3. Click the Fill Effects button.

   Excel displays the Fill Effects dialog box.

4. Select one of the four tabs (Gradient, Texture, Pattern, or Picture), depending on the kind of fill effect that you want to apply. The Picture tab, in particular, enables you to use a picture from an image file as your fill effect.

5. Specify the type of fill that you want. You have many options to choose from, and they're all quite straightforward.

6. Click OK twice to close the dialog boxes.

Changing a Chart's Data Series

Often, you create a chart that uses a particular range of data, and then you extend the data range by adding new data in the worksheet. If you add new data to a range, the data series in the chart doesn't update to include the new data. Or, you may delete some of the data in a range that you used to create the chart. If you delete data from a range, the chart displays the deleted data as zero values.

To update the chart to reflect the new data range, follow these steps:

1. Activate the chart, as we describe at the beginning of this part.

2. Choose Chart⇨Source Data.

3. In the Source Data dialog box that appears, select the Series tab.

4. Select the data series that you want to modify from the Series list box.

5. In the Values text box, edit the range to reflect the new range, or delete the range and select a new range in the worksheet by using the mouse pointer.

6. If necessary, modify the range in the Category (X) Axis Labels text box by using either of the methods that we describe in the preceding step.

7. Click OK, and Excel updates the chart with the new data range.

In Step 3, you can also select the Data Range tab of the Source Data dialog box and specify the data range for the entire chart by using either of the methods that we describe in Step 5.

After you activate a chart, Excel outlines in the worksheet the ranges that the chart uses. To extend or reduce the range, simply drag the handle on the outline in the worksheet.

A better way to handle data ranges that change is to use *named ranges*. Simply create names for the data ranges that you use in the chart. Activate the chart, select the data series, and edit the SERIES formula by clicking the Formula Bar. Replace each range reference with the corresponding range name. If you change the definition for a name, Excel updates the chart.

Changing a Chart's Location

If you embed your chart in a worksheet, you can click a border and drag the chart to a new location in the worksheet. To move the embedded chart to a different sheet or to a separate chart sheet, select the chart and choose Chart⇨Location. Specify the new location in the Chart Location dialog box, and click OK.

Changing Chart Elements

The following sections describe how to change chart elements, such as scale, gridlines, and data markers.

Changing a chart's scale

Adjusting the scale of a value axis can have a dramatic effect on the appearance of the chart. Excel always determines the scale for your charts automatically. You can, however, override Excel's choice by following these steps:

1. Activate the chart, as we describe at the beginning of this part.

2. Click the value (Y) axis, or select Value Axis from the drop-down list box on the Chart toolbar.

3. Choose Format⇨Selected Axis (or double-click the axis). You can also right-click the axis and choose Format Axis from the shortcut menu that appears.

4. In the Format Axis dialog box that appears, click the Scale tab.

5. Make the desired changes by selecting or deselecting the various options on the Scale tab and entering new values in the corresponding text boxes.

6. Click OK.

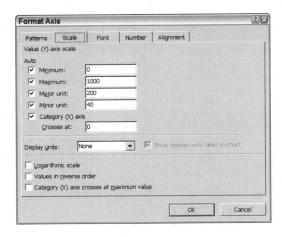

Remember: The dialog box varies slightly depending on which axis you select.

The Scale tab of the Format Axis dialog box offers the following options:

✔ **Minimum:** Enables you to enter a minimum value for the axis. If you select this check box, Excel determines this value automatically.

✔ **Maximum:** Enables you to enter a maximum value for the axis. If you select this check box, Excel determines this value automatically.

✔ **Major Unit:** Enables you to enter the number of units between major tick marks. If you select this check box, Excel determines this value automatically.

✔ **Minor Unit:** Enables you to enter the number of units between minor tick marks. If you select this check box, Excel determines this value automatically.

✔ **<Axis Type> Axis Crosses at:** Enables you to position the axes at a different location. By default, Excel positions the axes at the edge of the plot area. *<Axis Type>* can be either Category X or Value Y, depending on which axis you select.

✔ **Display Units:** Enables you to set the display units for large numbers on the axis. Using this option can make numbers appearing on the axis shorter and more readable.

✔ **Show Display Units Label on Chart:** Enables you to add a label on the axis that describes the units that you select in the Display Units drop-down list box.

✔ **Logarithmic Scale:** Enables you to use a logarithmic scale for the axes. This is useful for scientific applications in which the values that you want to plot have an extremely large range; a log scale gives you an error message if the scale includes zero or negative values.

✔ **Values in Reverse Order:** Makes the scale values extend in the opposite direction.

✔ **<Axis Type> Crosses at Maximum Value:** Enables you to position the axes at the maximum value of the perpendicular axis. (Normally, Excel positions the axis at the minimum value.) *<Axis Type>* can be either Category X or Value Y, depending on which axis you select.

Changing a chart's gridlines

Gridlines can help you determine what the chart series represents numerically. Gridlines simply extend the tick marks on the axes.

To add or remove gridlines, follow these steps:

1. Activate the chart.

2. Choose Chart⇨Chart Options.

   Excel displays the Chart Options dialog box.

3. Click the Gridlines tab.

4. Select or deselect the check boxes that correspond to the gridlines that you want. A preview window in the dialog box shows you how the gridlines appear on the chart.

Remember: Each axis has two sets of gridlines: major and minor. *Major units* are the ones that display a label. *Minor units* are those units that are in between the major units. If you're working with a 3-D chart, the dialog box has options for three sets of gridlines. [The third set is for the value (Z) axis.]

To modify the properties of a set of gridlines, follow these steps:

1. Activate the chart.

2. Select one gridline in the Minor or Major set of the axis of the gridlines that you want to modify.

3. Choose Format⇨Selected Gridlines (or double-click a gridline). You can also right-click the gridline and choose Format Gridlines from the shortcut menu that appears.

4. In the Format Gridlines dialog box that appears, select the Patterns tab and change the line style, weight, and color by choosing your options from the corresponding drop-down list boxes.

5. In the Format Gridlines dialog box, select the Scale tab to make adjustments to the scale that you use on the axis, and then click OK.

See also "Changing a chart's scale," immediately preceding in this part.

Changing data markers

Excel enables you to control various properties of data markers, such as size, style, and color. (A *data marker* is a symbol in a line, radar, or XY chart that Excel uses to represent a data point.) To control data marker properties, follow these steps:

1. Activate the chart (line chart, radar, or XY chart only), and double-click a data series in the chart.

   You can also right-click the data series and choose Format Data Series from the shortcut menu, or click the data series and choose Format⇨Selected Data Series.

   Excel displays the Format Data Series dialog box.

2. Select the Patterns tab. (This tab is the default, so it may already be selected as the dialog box opens.)

3. In the Marker area of the dialog box, make your changes, as follows: Click a radio button to specify the type of marker (Automatic, None, or Custom). If you select the Custom option, you can choose a style and/or color from the corresponding drop-down list boxes and enter a size for the marker in the Size

text box. The Sample area shows how the marker appears on the chart.

4. Click OK to close the dialog box.

You can also use a graphic object or picture for the data markers. Copy the graphic object or picture to the Clipboard. Then select a marker in the chart, and choose Edit⇨Paste. You may need to experiment with various sizes.

Changing the Chart Type

Excel supports a wide variety of chart types (line charts, column charts, and so on).

To change the chart type, follow these steps:

1. Activate the chart.

2. Choose Chart⇨Chart Type to display the Chart Type dialog box.

3. Click the chart type that you want in the dialog box.

   You can select from standard chart types (on the Standard tab) or custom chart types (on the Custom tab). You see a preview of how your chart will look.

4. After you're satisfied with the chart's appearance, click OK.

The chart types that appear in the Custom tab of the Chart Type dialog box are standard chart types that are modified in one or more ways. Excel comes with a variety of custom chart types, and you can also create your own.

Another way to change the chart type is to use the Chart Type tool on the Chart toolbar. This tool displays the major chart types in the tool's pull-down menu. (You can't select custom chart types if you use this tool.)

If you customize some aspects of your chart, choosing a new chart type may override some of or all the changes you make. For example, if you add gridlines to the chart and then select a chart type that doesn't use gridlines, your gridlines disappear.

See also "Creating a Custom Chart Type," later in this part.

Creating a Chart by Using the Chart Wizard

The Chart Wizard consists of a series of four dialog boxes that prompt you for various settings for the chart. By the time that you reach the last dialog box, the chart is usually exactly what you need. To use the Chart Wizard to create a chart, follow these steps:

1. Before you open the Chart Wizard, select the data that you want to include in the chart. In your selection, include items such as labels and series identifiers.

   The data that you're plotting doesn't need to be contiguous. You can press and hold Ctrl while making multiple selections.

2. After selecting the data, open the Chart Wizard by clicking the Chart Wizard button on the Standard toolbar or by choosing Insert⇨Chart.

Excel displays the first Chart Wizard dialog box.

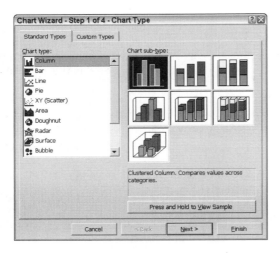

Remember: While using the Chart Wizard, you can go back to the previous step by clicking the Back button. Or you can click Finish to end the Chart Wizard. If you end it early, Excel creates the chart using the information that you provide up to that point.

Chart Wizard — Dialog box 1 of 4

The first step of the Chart Wizard involves selecting the chart type. To do so, follow these steps:

1. Select the chart type. To use a standard chart type, make your selection in the Chart Type list box on the Standard Types tab. Then click one of the chart subtypes in the Chart Sub-type area. To use a custom chart type, make your selection in the Custom Types tab.

To get a preview of how your data looks with the selected chart type, use the button below the list of chart subtypes. Click the button, but don't release it.

2. Click the Next button to move to the next dialog box.

Chart Wizard — Dialog box 2 of 4

In the second dialog box of the Chart Wizard, you verify (or change) the ranges that are used in the chart. To do so, follow these steps:

1. Make sure that the range that appears in the Data range text box is the range that you want to use for the chart.

2. If the data series are in rows, click the Rows option button. If the data series are in columns, select the Columns option button.

   The dialog box displays a preview of the chart.

3. To adjust the ranges that you're using for an individual series, click the Series tab and make the appropriate changes. (*See* "Changing a Chart's Data Series," earlier in this part, for details.)

4. Click the Next button to proceed to the next step.

Remember: The row or column selection in Step 2 is an important choice that has a drastic effect on the look of your chart. Most of the time, Excel guesses the data orientation correctly — but not always.

Chart Wizard — Dialog box 3 of 4

The third Chart Wizard dialog box consists of six tabs. Use these tabs to adjust various options for the chart. As you make your selections, the preview chart reflects your choices. The tabs in this dialog box of the wizard are as follows:

✔ **Titles:** Enter titles for various parts of the chart on this tab.

✔ **Axes:** Select the type of values to display on the axes on this tab.

✔ **Gridlines:** Specify gridlines, if any, on this tab.

✔ **Legend:** Specify whether to display a legend and indicate its location in the chart on this tab.

✔ **Data Labels:** Specify whether to display data labels (and which type) for the data series on this tab.

✔ **Data Table:** Specify whether to display a table of values that the chart uses on this tab.

See also "Changing Chart Elements," "Adding a legend to a chart," "Displaying a Data Table in a Chart," and "Displaying Data Labels in a Chart," elsewhere in this part.

Click Next to move to the final dialog box of the Chart Wizard.

Chart Wizard — Dialog box 4 of 4

In the final dialog box of the Chart Wizard, you specify where you want the chart to appear. You can display it as a new chart sheet or as an object in an existing worksheet. (You can select the sheet.)

After you click Finish, Excel creates the chart per your specifications.

Remember: You can always change any aspect of the chart by using the procedures that we describe elsewhere in this part. Or, you can activate the chart and click the Chart Wizard button to modify an existing chart.

Creating a Custom Chart Type

Excel offers quite a few custom chart types; you can also create your own user-defined chart type. You can apply a custom chart type that you create to any other chart by following these steps:

1. Create a chart that's customized the way that you want.

   For example, you can set any of the colors or line styles, change the scales, modify fonts and type sizes, add gridlines, add a title, and even add free-floating text or graphic images.

2. Activate the chart, and choose Chart➪Chart Type.

3. In the Chart Type dialog box that appears, click the Custom Types tab.

4. Click the User-Defined option button.

5. Click the Add button to add a new custom chart type, basing it on the current chart.

   Another dialog box appears.

6. In the Add Custom Chart Type dialog box, type a name for the chart type in the top text box and a description in the bottom text box.

   The custom chart type name that you supply now appears in the Custom Types tab of the Chart Type dialog box. Notice that you must click the User-Defined option button for user-defined chart types to appear.

7. Click OK to return to the Chart Type dialog box, and then click OK again to return to your chart.

Creating a Default Chart on a Chart Sheet

If you intend to print a chart on a page by itself or if have many charts to create in the same workbook, your best choice is to use a chart sheet.

To quickly create a chart on a new chart sheet, follow these steps:

1. Select the worksheet data that you want to chart.

2. Press F11.

Excel inserts a new chart sheet and displays the chart, basing it on the selected data. Excel creates its default chart type by using the default settings.

Remember: For more control over the chart-making process, use the Chart Wizard.

See also "Creating a Chart by Using the Chart Wizard," earlier in this part.

Deleting a Chart Element or Data Series

You can delete any element in a chart.

To delete a chart element, follow these steps:

1. Select the element or data series that you want to delete.

2. Press Delete.

See also "Selecting a Chart Element," later in this part.

Remember: If you delete the last data series in a chart, the chart is considered to be empty.

Displaying a Data Table in a Chart

In Excel, you can display a table of the data that you use in the chart. The data table appears below the chart. If you create the chart by using the Chart Wizard, you can add the data table in Step 3. (***See*** "Chart Wizard — Dialog box 3 of 4," earlier in this part, for details.) To add a data table to an existing chart, follow these steps:

1. Activate the chart.

2. Choose Chart⇨Chart Options. You can also right-click the border area of the chart and select Chart Options from the shortcut menu.

Excel displays its Chart Options dialog box.

3. Click the Data Table tab.

4. Select the Show Data Table check box.

5. Depending on your preference for displaying legend keys on the data table, select or deselect the Show Legend Keys check box.

6. Click OK. The data table appears below the chart.

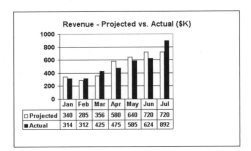

To change the line color or font for the data table, double-click the table and make the appropriate changes in the Format Data Table dialog box that appears.

Displaying Data Labels in a Chart

Sometimes, you want your chart to display the actual data values for each point on the chart. Or, you may want to display the category (X-axis) label for each data point.

To add data labels to a chart series, follow these steps:

1. Activate the chart.

2. Click one of the data points in the series. This action selects the entire data series.

   Be careful not to click a data point after you select the entire series, because this action selects only a single data point. If you accidentally select a single data point, click anywhere outside the data series and repeat the step.

3. Choose Format➪Selected Data Series (or double-click the data series in the chart). You can also right-click a data point and choose Format Data Series from the shortcut menu that appears.

4. In the Format Data Series dialog box that appears, click the Data Labels tab.

5. Select the option or options that correspond to the type of data labels that you want to display on the chart. You can

display the Series name, Category name (horizontal or X-axis name), Value (vertical or Y-axis value), Percentage (for pie and doughnut charts only), Bubble size (for bubble charts only), and Legend key.

If you want to display more than one option, you can choose a separator from the Separator drop-down list box.

6. Click OK. The data labels appear on the chart.

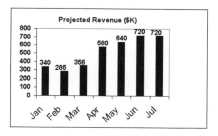

Remember: The data labels link to the worksheet, so if your data changes, the labels also change. To override the data label with some other text, select the label and enter the new text (or even a cell reference) in the Formula Bar.

 If Excel doesn't position the data labels correctly, you can select an individual label and move it to a better location by dragging it. To select an individual label, click the label twice.

Remember: You can't specify a range of text to use as data labels. Data labels can consist of either data values or category (X) axis labels. You must add data labels and then edit each one manually.

Formatting a Chart Element

You can modify most elements in a chart in several ways. For example, you can change colors, line widths, fonts, and so on. You make modifications in the Format dialog box (which varies for each type of chart element).

To modify an element in a chart, follow these steps:

1. Select the chart element. (**See** "Selecting a Chart Element," later in this part, for details.)

2. Access the Format dialog box for the chart element that you select by using any of the following techniques:

- Double-click the item.

- Choose Format⇨Selected [*Item Name*], where [*Item Name*] is the name of the chart element that you select — for example, Data Series, Gridlines, Axis, and so on.

- Press Ctrl+1.

- Right-click the item, and choose Format [*Item Name*] from the shortcut menu that appears. [*Item Name*] is the name of the chart element you select — for example, Data Series, Gridlines, Axis, and so on.

3. Click the tab on the dialog box that corresponds to what you want to do.

4. Make the changes by selecting the appropriate options.

   To get help on an option, click the Help button (the question mark) in the dialog box to display the Help window and click the option link (blue text) to reveal details on the option.

   See also "Changing data markers" and "Displaying Data Labels in a Chart," earlier in this part.

5. Click OK.

Handling Missing Data in a Chart

Sometimes, data that you're charting may be missing one or more data points. Excel offers several options for handling the missing data. Just follow these steps:

1. Activate the chart.

2. Choose Tools⇨Options.

3. In the Options dialog box that appears, click the Chart tab.

4. Select the option that corresponds to how you want to handle the missing data.

   The available radio button options are as follows:

   - **Not Plotted (Leave Gaps):** Excel simply ignores missing data, and the data series leaves a gap for each missing data point.

   - **Zero:** Excel treats missing data as zero.

   - **Interpolated:** Excel calculates missing data by using data on either side of the missing point(s). This option is available only for line charts.

Remember: The options that you set apply to the entire active chart; you can't set a different option for different series in the same chart.

Inserting and Modifying Chart Legends

A *legend* explains the data series in a chart. A legend consists of text and *keys*. A key is a small graphic that corresponds to the chart's series. The following figure, for example, shows a chart with the legend keys Projected and Actual.

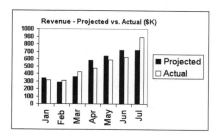

Adding a legend to a chart

If you create your chart by using the Chart Wizard, you can include a legend. (See Step 3 in the following steps.) If you don't include a legend as you create the chart, you can add one later if you need one. To add a legend, follow these steps:

1. Activate the chart.

2. Choose Chart⇨Chart Options. You can also right-click the border area of the chart and select Chart Options from the shortcut menu.

   Excel displays its Chart Options dialog box.

3. Click the Legend tab.

4. Select the Show Legend check box.

5. Select a placement option for the legend by clicking the appropriate radio button: Bottom, Corner, Top, Right, or Left.

   The picture of the chart in the Legend tab displays how the legend appears on the chart for various placement options.

6. Click OK.

Adding titles to a chart legend

If you don't include legend text as you originally select the cells to create the chart, Excel displays *Series 1, Series 2,* and so on in the legend. To add series names or titles, follow these steps:

1. Activate the chart.

2. Choose Chart⇨Source Data. You can also right-click the border area of the chart and select Source Data from the shortcut menu.

3. In the Source Data dialog box that appears, click the Series tab.

4. Select a series from the Series list box, and then enter a name in the Name text box. For the name, you can use text or a reference to a cell that contains the series name.

5. Repeat Step 4 for each series that you want to name.

6. Click OK, and the new names appear in the legend.

Formatting a chart legend or legend entry

After you create a legend for a chart, you may want to add various formatting options to the legend or specific legend entries. To format a chart legend, perform the following steps:

1. Select the chart legend.

2. Choose Format⇨Selected Legend, or right-click the legend and choose Format Legend from the shortcut menu that appears.

3. In the Format Legend dialog box that appears, select a tab and then select the appropriate options in the tab.

   The options in the Patterns tab, for example, enable you to select the type of border (if any) and background color/shading for the legend.

To format a specific legend entry, perform the following steps:

1. Select the chart legend.

2. Select the legend entry that you want to format by clicking the legend text.

3. Choose Format⇨Selected Legend Entry, or right-click the legend entry and choose Format Legend Entry from the shortcut menu that appears.

4. Make the appropriate formatting changes in the Format Legend Entry dialog box.

5. Click OK.

Moving a Chart Element

You can move some of the chart parts (any of the titles, the data labels, and the legend). To move a chart element, follow these steps:

1. Select the chart element that you want to move.

2. Click the border of the element, and drag the element to the desired location in the chart.

See also "Selecting a Chart Element," later in this part.

Rotating 3-D Charts

As you work with 3-D charts, you may find that some data is completely or partially obscured. You can rotate the chart so that it shows the data better by following these steps:

1. Activate the 3-D chart.

2. Choose Chart⇨3-D View.

3. In the 3-D View dialog box that appears, make your rotations and perspective changes by clicking the appropriate controls.

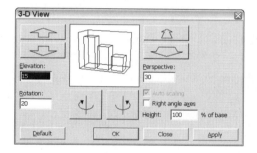

4. Click OK (or click Apply to see the changes without closing the dialog box).

You can also rotate the chart in real time by dragging corners with the mouse. Normally, this procedure displays an outline of the chart's borders only. If you press and hold Ctrl while dragging a corner, you can also see outlines of the chart series.

Selecting a Chart Element

Modifying an element in a chart is similar to everything else that you do in Excel: First you make a selection (in this case, selecting a chart part), and then you issue a command to do something with the selection.

After you activate a chart, you can select a chart element in any of the following three ways:

✔ Click the chart element. If the element is a series, clicking the series once selects all the points in the series. Clicking the series twice selects individual points in the series.

✔ Press the up-arrow or down-arrow key to cycle through all the elements in the chart. If a data series is selected, you can press the right-arrow or left-arrow key to select individual points in the series.

✔ Use the Chart Objects control in the Chart toolbar. This control is a drop-down list that contains all the elements in the chart.

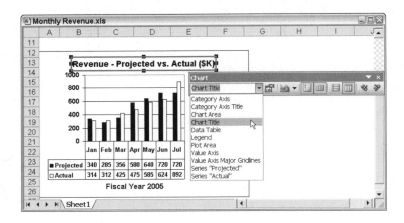

Regardless of which method you use, the name of the selected item appears in the Name text box (at the left of the Formula Bar). Many of the chart element names include a number that further describes the element. The third point of the first data series, for example, is named Series 1 Point 3. You can't change the names of chart elements, and you can't select more than one element at a time.

If you move the mouse pointer over a chart element, a chart tip displays the name of the element. If the element is a data point, the chart tip displays the value. To control what appears in these chart tips, select Tools➪Options and click the Chart tab. Make your selection in the Chart tips area of the dialog box.

Linking and Consolidating Worksheets

Linking and consolidation are two procedures that are common in the world of spreadsheets. *Linking* is the process of using references to cells in external workbooks to get data into your worksheet. *Consolidation* combines or summarizes information from two or more worksheets (which can be in multiple workbooks).

In this part . . .

Consolidating Worksheets

Data consolidation refers to the process of merging data from multiple worksheets or multiple workbook files. A division manager, for example, may consolidate various departmental budgets into a single workbook.

Whether you lay out the information exactly the same way in each worksheet is the main factor that determines the ease of a consolidation task. If you do so, the job proves to be relatively simple.

If the worksheets have little or no resemblance to each other, your best bet may be to edit each sheet so that they match each other. In some cases, simply reentering the information in a standard format may prove to be more efficient than editing each sheet.

Any of the following techniques enable you to consolidate information from multiple worksheets or workbooks:

   ✔ Use formulas (link formulas if the data is in multiple workbooks).

   ✔ Choose Data⇨Consolidate.

   ✔ Use a PivotTable.

See also Part XIII.

Consolidating by position or by matching labels

If you lay out the worksheets that you want to consolidate identically, the data in the rows and columns of each worksheet appears in the same location, making the consolidation task straightforward. If, on the other hand, you don't lay out the worksheets that you want to consolidate identically, you can still consolidate the worksheets, but only if the worksheets contain identical row and column labels. In this case, Excel uses the row and column labels to match the data.

If you lay out your worksheets identically or if the worksheets contain identical row and column labels, follow these steps to consolidate the data from the worksheets:

   1. Start with a new workbook. (*See* "The Basics: Creating an Empty Workbook File," in The Big Picture part, for details.)

   The source workbooks can be open, but this isn't necessary.

   2. Choose Data⇨Consolidate to open the Consolidate dialog box.

   3. Select the type of consolidation summary that you want from the Function drop-down list box.

   Most of the time, you use Sum, which adds the corresponding values together.

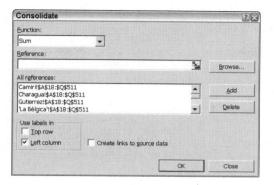

4. Enter the range reference for the first worksheet in the Reference text box.

   If the workbook is open, you can click the Reference text box and select the worksheet range by using the mouse pointer. If it's not open, click the Browse button to locate the file on your hard drive, network drive, and so on. The reference must include a range. After the reference in the Reference text box is correct, click Add to add it to the All References list box.

5. Repeat Step 4 for each additional worksheet that you want to consolidate.

6. If you laid out the worksheets identically, you can skip to Step 7.

   If you didn't lay out the worksheets in the same way, you must select the Left Column and Top Row check boxes to match the data by using the labels in the worksheet.

7. If you select the Create links to source data check box, Excel creates linked references to individual cells in each of the consolidating ranges. All corresponding cells across the ranges are grouped and totaled (assuming that you select Sum in Step 3) in the form of an outline.

8. Click OK to begin the consolidation.

Consolidating by using formulas

You can consolidate information across worksheets by creating formulas that refer to cells in the source worksheets. To consolidate data by using formulas, perform the following steps:

1. Start with an empty worksheet.

2. Enter a formula that uses the cells in each of the source worksheets. (This task is much easier if all the workbooks are open.)

3. If you lay out the source worksheets identically, copy the formula that you create in Step 2 to create summary formulas for other cells.

   If the source worksheets have different layouts, you need to create each formula separately.

Remember: Using formulas in this manner ensures that Excel updates the consolidation formulas if the source data changes.

See also "Referencing cells in other workbooks," later in this part, and "Referencing Cells in Other Worksheets," in Part IV.

Linking Workbooks

By using *linking,* you join worksheets so that one depends on the other. The workbook that contains the link formulas (or external reference formulas) is the *destination* workbook. The workbook that is the source of the information that the external reference formula uses is the *source* workbook. Notice that the source workbook doesn't need to remain open while the destination workbook is open.

Referencing cells in other workbooks

If your formula needs to refer to a cell in a different workbook, use the following format for your formula:

```
=[WorkbookName]SheetName!CellAddress
```

The workbook name (in brackets), the worksheet name, and an exclamation point precede the cell address. Such a formula is sometimes known as a *link formula* or an *external reference.*

Remember: If the workbook name in the reference includes one or more spaces, you must enclose the workbook name and the sheet name in single quotation marks. The following formula, for example, refers to a cell in Sheet1 in a workbook named Budget For 2005:

```
=A1*'[Budget For 2005]Sheet1'!A1
```

If a formula refers to cells in a different workbook, the other workbook doesn't need to remain open. If the workbook is closed, you must add the complete path to the reference. An example is as follows:

```
=A1* 'C:\My Documents\Excel\[Budget For
2005]Sheet1'!A1
```

 The easiest way to enter formulas that require external links is by pointing. To do this, you must have all source workbooks open. *See also* "Entering formulas by pointing," in Part III.

To avoid problems that can occur in formulas on the dependent workbook when you insert or delete rows, columns, or cells or otherwise move linked cells or ranges in source workbooks, we strongly recommend that you use names for cells or ranges that the dependent workbook references in the source workbooks.

Changing the source of links

If your workbook uses one or more formulas that contain links to other workbooks, you may need to change the source workbook for your external references. You may, for example, have a worksheet with links to a workbook named Preliminary Budget. Later, you get a finalized version named Final Budget.

To change the link source, follow these steps:

1. Choose Edit➪Links.

2. In the Edit Links dialog box that appears, click the source workbook that you want to change from the list.

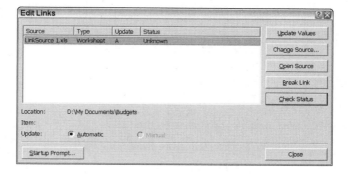

3. Click the Change Source button.

4. In the Change Source dialog box that appears, select a new source file and then click OK.

5. Click the Close button to exit the Edit Links dialog box.

After you select the file, all external reference formulas update.

Severing (breaking) links

If you have external references in a workbook (that is, links to a different workbook) and then decide that you don't want them, you can convert the external reference formulas to values, thereby severing the links.

Follow these steps to break the links to an external workbook:

1. Choose Edit⇨Links.

2. In the Edit Links dialog box that appears, click the source workbook for which you want to break all links.

3. Click the Break Link button.

   Excel provides a dialog box that asks you to confirm your request.

4. Click the Break Links button in the confirmation dialog box.

   All references to the source workbook convert to their current values.

5. Click the Close button to exit the Edit Links dialog box.

Updating links

To ensure that your link formulas have the latest values from their source workbooks, you can force an update. Forcing an update may prove necessary if you've just discovered that an updated version of a source workbook was saved to your network server.

To update linked formulas with their current values, follow these steps:

1. Choose Edit⇨Links.

2. In the Edit Links dialog box that appears, choose the appropriate source workbook from the list.

3. Click the Update Values button.

   Excel updates the link formulas.

4. Click the Close button to exit the Edit Links dialog box.

Remember: By default, every time that you open a workbook with links to other workbooks, Excel prompts you with a request to update the links if any of the source workbooks are not already open. If you want Excel to update the workbook automatically without a prompt, choose Tools⇨Options, select the Edit tab in the Options dialog box, and clear the Ask to update automatic links check box.

Working with Lists and External Data

A *list* is an organized collection of information. A list consists of a row of headers (descriptive text), followed by additional rows of data, which can be values or text. External data refers to information foreign to Excel's native file formats; this data can be in the form of a database or at least in a format that enables you to easily import it into Excel's rows and columns for analysis.

In this part . . .

You can store information of just about any type in a *list.* If you're familiar with the concept of a *database table,* you recognize that a list has many similarities, as follows:

✔ Columns correspond to fields.

✔ Rows correspond to records.

✔ The first row of the table should have field names that describe the data in each column.

Furthermore, a list can have no empty rows or columns, because Excel uses empty rows and columns to delimit the boundaries of a list.

	A	B	C	D	E	F	G
8	Date	Amount	AcctType	OpenedBy	Branch	Customer	
9	6/1/2004	340	Checking	New Accts	Central	Existing	
10	6/1/2004	15,759	CD	Teller	Westside	Existing	
11	6/1/2004	15,276	CD	New Accts	North County	Existing	
12	6/1/2004	12,000	CD	New Accts	Westside	Existing	
13	6/1/2004	5,000	CD	New Accts	North County	Existing	
14	6/1/2004	7,000	Savings	New Accts	North County	New	
15	6/1/2004	90,000	CD	New Accts	Central	Existing	
16	6/1/2004	124	Checking	Teller	Central	Existing	
17	6/1/2004	400	Checking	Teller	Central	Existing	
18	6/1/2004	100	Checking	New Accts	Central	Existing	
19	6/1/2004	14,644	CD	New Accts	Westside	New	
20	6/1/2004	5,000	Savings	New Accts	Westside	Existing	
21	6/1/2004	4,623	Savings	New Accts	North County	Existing	
22	6/1/2004	5,879	Checking	New Accts	Central	Existing	
23	6/1/2004	3,171	Checking	New Accts	Westside	Existing	

account-db.xls — June

Select Window➪Freeze Panes to make sure that the headings are always visible as the list scrolls.

See also "Freezing Row or Column Titles," in Part II.

You can preform at entire columns to ensure that the data has the same format. If a column contains dates, for example, format the entire column in the date format that you want.

The List AutoFill feature automatically copies formatting and formulas as you add new rows below the last row in the list. You can toggle this feature by choosing Tools➪Options, clicking the Edit tab of the Options dialog box that appears, and selecting or deselecting the Extend List Formats and Formulas check box.

Remember: An Excel worksheet contains 65,536 rows, and a cell can hold no more than 32,000 characters.

Accessing Advanced Filtering

Advanced filtering is more flexible than autofiltering, but using it takes some up-front work. Advanced filtering provides you with the following capabilities:

✔ You can specify more complex filtering criteria.

✔ You can specify computed filtering criteria.

✔ You can extract a copy of the rows that meet the criteria to another location.

See also "Filtering a List," later in this part.

Setting up a criteria range for advanced filtering

Before you can use the Advanced Filtering feature, you must set up a *criteria range* — an area in a worksheet that holds the information that Excel uses to filter the list. The criteria range must conform to the following specifications:

✔ The criteria range must consist of at least two rows.

✔ The first row must contain some or all of the field names from the list.

✔ The other rows must consist of filtering criteria.

If you use more than one criterion in a row of a criteria range, Excel filters the records that meet all criteria *simultaneously*. If you use more than one row below the field names in the criteria range, Excel filters the records that meet the criteria set in each row.

The entries that you make in a criteria range can be either of the following:

✔ **Text or value criteria:** The filtering involves comparisons to a value or text, using operators such as equal to (=), greater than (>), not equal to (<>), and so on.

The following table shows examples of text criteria.

Criterion	Effect
>K	Text that begins with *L* through *Z*
<>C	All text, except text that begins with *C*
January	Text that matches *January*
sm*	Text that begins with *sm*
s*s	Text that begins with *s* and ends with *s*
s?s	Three-letter text that begins with *s* and ends with *s*

Remember: The text comparisons aren't case sensitive. The text criterion *si**, for example, matches *Simon* as well as *sick*.

✔ **Computed criteria:** The filtering involves some sort of computation.

Computed criteria filters the list based on one or more calculations and *does not* use a field header from the list. Computed criteria require you to specify a new (or blank) field name in the criteria range header row.

Computed criteria is a logical formula (returning True or False) that refers to cells in the first row of data in the list, that is, the row immediately below the header row.

Performing advanced filtering

To perform advanced filtering on a list, follow these steps:

1. Set up a criteria range. *See* "Setting up a criteria range for advanced filtering," immediately preceding in this part.

2. Click anywhere in the list.

3. Choose Data➪Filter➪Advanced Filter.

Excel displays the Advanced Filter dialog box. By clicking in the list in Step 2, Excel automatically selects the list range in the List Range box.

4. In the Advanced Filter dialog box, click in the Criteria Range box and select the criteria range you set up in Step 1.

5. To filter the list in its present location, select the Filter the list, in-place radio button. Otherwise, to extract the filtered data to another location in the worksheet, select the Copy to Another Location radio button and specify the copy location.

6. To filter out (hide) duplicate records that meet your criteria, select the Unique records only check box.

7. Click OK, and Excel filters the list according to the criteria that you specify.

See also "Filtering a List," later in this part.

Applying Database Functions with Lists

To create a formula that returns results based on filtered criteria, you can use the Excel database worksheet functions. For example, you can create a formula that calculates the sum of values in a list that meets certain criteria. To use a database function, follow these steps:

1. Set up a criteria range in your worksheet.

2. Enter a formula such as the following:

```
=DSUM(Database,Field,Criteria)
```

In this case, *Database* refers to the list, *Field* refers to the field name (header) cell of the column being summed, and *Criteria* refers to the criteria range.

To see a list of available database functions, use the Insert Function dialog box and select Database from the category drop-down list box. You can see a list of database functions in the Select a function list box. **See** "Using the Insert Function dialog box," in Part IV.

See also "Setting up a criteria range for advanced filtering," earlier in this part.

Calculating Subtotals

Excel has the capability to create subtotal formulas automatically; this is handy and can save you lots of time. The formulas all use the Subtotal worksheet function to insert the subtotals. To use the subtotal feature, you must have a list that's sorted. **See also** "Sorting a List," later in this part, for details.

To insert subtotal formulas into a list, follow these steps:

1. Move the cell pointer anywhere in the list.

2. Choose Data⇨Subtotals from the menu bar.

3. Complete the Subtotal dialog box that appears by specifying the options in the appropriate check and drop-down list boxes. To get help on an option, click the dialog box's Help button (the question mark) to display the Help window and click the option link (blue text) to reveal details on the option.

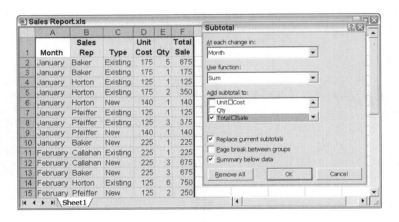

4. Click OK, and Excel analyzes the list and inserts formulas as specified — and creates an outline for you.

Filtering a List

Excel enables you to filter lists either by using an Excel AutoFilter or by setting up a custom AutoFilter of your own, as the following sections describe.

Filtering by using an Excel AutoFilter

Autofiltering enables you to view only certain rows in your list by hiding rows that don't qualify based on criteria that you set.

To AutoFilter a list, follow these steps:

1. Move the cell pointer anywhere within the list.

2. Choose Data⇨Filter⇨AutoFilter.

   Excel analyzes your list and then adds drop-down arrows to the field names in the header row.

3. Click the arrow on one of these drop-down lists.

   The drop-down list shows the unique items in that column.

4. Select an item.

   Excel hides all rows except those that include the selected item. In other words, it filters the list by the item that you selected.

   In addition to the unique items in a column, the drop-down list includes the following five other items:

   - **All:** Displays all items in the column. Use this setting to remove filtering for a column.

   - **Top 10:** Filters to display the "top 10" items in the list. Actually, you can display any number of the top (or bottom) values.

   - **Custom:** Enables you to filter the list by multiple items.

   - **Blanks:** Filters the list by showing only rows that contain blanks in this column.

   - **NonBlanks:** Filters the list by showing only rows that contain nonblanks in this column.

The Blanks and NonBlanks options are available only if the column that you want to filter contains a blank cell.

Remember: After you filter the list, the status bar displays a message that tells you how many rows qualify. In addition, the drop-down arrow changes color to remind you that Excel is filtering the list by a value in that column.

To display the entire list again, choose Data⇨Filter⇨Show All.

To get out of AutoFilter mode and remove the drop-down arrows from the field names, choose Data⇨Filter⇨AutoFilter again.

See also "Accessing Advanced Filtering," earlier in this part, and "Filtering by using a custom AutoFilter," immediately following in this part.

Filtering by using a custom AutoFilter

Normally, autofiltering involves selecting a single value for one or more columns. Excel then filters the list by that value. For more flexibility, choose the Custom option in an AutoFilter drop-down list to open the Custom AutoFilter dialog box.

The Custom AutoFilter dialog box enables you to filter by using up to two sets of criteria. Follow these steps after opening the Custom AutoFilter dialog box:

1. Select the filtering operation for the first criteria set (equals, is greater than, is less than, and so on) from the upper-left drop-down list box.

2. Enter a value or text (depending on whether you have values or text in the column that you're filtering) in the upper-right combination drop-down list/text box. You can also select an item from the drop-down list. The list contains all the unique items in the column that you're filtering.

3. To add another criteria set, click the And or Or radio button.

4. Repeat Steps 1 and 2, but use the lower-left and -right drop-down list boxes to enter the second criteria set.

5. Click OK.

   Excel filters the list based on your chosen criteria.

Custom autofiltering is useful, but it has limitations. For example, to filter the list to show only three values in a field (such as January or April or June), you can't do it by using autofiltering. Such filtering tasks require the Advanced Filter feature.

See also "Filtering by using a custom AutoFilter," and "Accessing Advanced Filtering," both earlier in this part.

Importing Data from a Text File

Very often, the data that you want to import into Excel for analysis is in the multiple rows and columns of a text file. Importing such data can often prove tricky, because the rows and columns don't always line up easily to fit into Excel's row-and-column structure (as is the case if multiple delimiters — for example, spaces and commas — separate the data in a random manner). Excel, however, provides a Text Import Wizard, which makes importing such text data relatively easy.

To import a text file into Excel, follow these steps:

1. Choose Data⇨Import External Data⇨Import Data. This command opens the Select Data Source dialog box.

2. In the Look In drop-down list box, navigate to the folder in which the text file resides.

3. If the text file that you're importing doesn't have one of Excel's recognized extensions (TXT, PRN, CSV, and so on), select the All Files option in the Files of Type drop-down list box.

4. Select the file, and click Open.

   Excel examines the file and performs the following actions:

   - If the file is a tab-delimited or a comma-separated value (CSV) file, Excel often imports it with no further intervention on your part. You can skip to Step 6.

   - If you can import the file in several different ways or if it contains no delimiters, Excel displays the first step of its Text Import Wizard. Continue on with Step 5.

5. In Step 1 of 3 of the Text Import Wizard, select Delimited or Fixed Width, depending on how the data in the text file is organized. If the data is separated with tabs or commas, Excel automatically selects the Delimited option.

   Click Next to proceed to Step 2 of 3 of the wizard.

6. In Step 2 of 3, select the appropriate delimiter if the one that Excel chooses is not suitable.

   The preview window at the bottom of the dialog box shows how Excel will import the data into its rows and columns. Excel shows vertical bars that separate the data it will import into multiple columns. If you do not see any vertical bars (or if the separation Excel chooses is not what you want), select a different delimiter.

   Click Next to proceed to Step 3 of 3 of the wizard.

7. In Step 3 of 3, click a data column in the preview window and select a format for the data. Repeat the procedure for the remaining columns.

If you leave the columns in the default general format, Excel chooses a format that is appropriate for each column of data.

8. Click Finish to complete the wizard. The Import Data dialog box now appears.

9. In the Import Data dialog box, select where you want to put the data and click OK to complete the import.

See also "Refreshing Imported Data," later in this part.

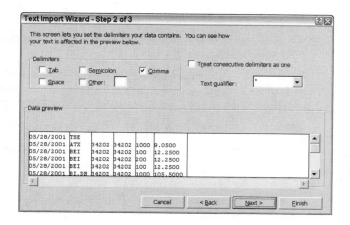

Importing Data from the Web

To analyze data on a Web page, such as stock quotes, you can use a Web query to retrieve a single table, multiple tables, or all the text on the Web page. After you retrieve the data, you can analyze it by using tools and features in Excel.

By using an existing Web query file

A *Web query file* is a special file that contains information about the data that you want to import. It may, for example, specify which tables on a Web page to import, the type of formatting to apply to the imported tables, and any parameters to include as you run the query. Excel saves Web query files with an IQY extension.

If a query is already defined, follow these steps to retrieve the data that you want:

1. Make sure that you're connected to the Web.

2. Activate a worksheet.

3. Choose Data⇨Import External Data⇨Import Data.

   Excel displays the Select Data Source dialog box.

4. In the Look In drop-down list box, navigate to the folder in which the Web query file resides.

5. Select the file, and click Open. The Import Data dialog box appears.

6. In the Import Data dialog box, specify where you want to put the data and click OK to complete the import.

Microsoft includes useful sample Web query files with Excel, such as files to retrieve stock quotes, major indices, and currency rates.

See also "By creating a new Web query," immediately following in this part, and "Refreshing Imported Data," later in this part.

By creating a new Web query

Before you create your own Web query, you need the address of the Web site from which you want to get the data.

To create a new Web query, follow these steps:

1. Make sure that you're connected to the Web.

2. Activate a worksheet.

3. Choose Data⇨Import External Data⇨New Web Query.

   Excel displays the New Web Query dialog box.

4. In the Address area of the New Web Query dialog box, type or paste an address for the Web page.

   Make sure that you enter the address of the Web page that contains the data and not the address of a frame or frames page.

5. After the Web page appears on-screen, choose the data that you want Excel to return by clicking the arrow image next to the data. A green check mark replaces the arrow.

   Use the arrow in the upper-left corner of the dialog box window to select the entire page. (Clicking it returns text, tables, and other data except graphic images.) You can select multiple tables if you want.

   If the arrows aren't visible, click the Show Icons button in the dialog box.

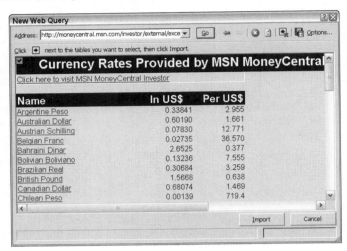

6. Click the Options button to change import settings. You can use the Web Query Options dialog box that appears to specify how much formatting you want to import from the Web page as well as other settings.

7. To save the query definition to a file so that you can retrieve the same data in other workbooks or share the query file with other users, click the Save Query button (which you find to the left of the Options button).

   Excel displays the Save Query dialog box. Provide a name and location for the query definition, and click Save. Excel saves Web query files with the IQY extension.

8. Click Import in the New Web Query dialog box. In the Import Data dialog box that appears, specify where you want to put the data and click OK to complete the import.

Remember: If you use the sample stock-quote query file that comes with Excel (MSN MoneyCentral Investor Stock Quotes.iqy), notice that you can enter a parameter value (the stock or fund symbols) as you run the query. The New Web Query dialog box doesn't enable you to create Web queries that prompt for parameters. To create this type of Web query, you need knowledge of Hypertext Markup Language (HTML), and the Web page must be set up to accept parameter input.

See also "By using an existing Web query file," earlier in this part, and Refreshing Imported Data," immediately following in this part.

Refreshing Imported Data

When you import data into Excel via the Data⇨Import External Data command, by default Excel saves the *query definition* (your import criteria) with the worksheet in which you import the data. Doing this allows you refresh (update) the worksheet when the source data changes, without having to repeat the import process from scratch. Excel provides the following options to enable you to refresh the data automatically or manually:

✔ To refresh your data automatically, use the Refresh control options in the External Data Range Properties dialog box.

✔ To refresh your data at any time, right-click anywhere inside the imported data range and choose Refresh External Data from the shortcut menu or click the Refresh External Data button on the External Data toolbar.

Sorting a List

Sorting a list involves rearranging the rows so that they're in ascending or descending order, based on the values in one or more columns. You may, for example, want to sort a list of salespeople alphabetically by last name or by sales region. You can sort either numerically or alphabetically, depending on the data. In some cases, you may want to sort your data in other ways. If your data consists of month names, for example, you probably want them to appear in month order rather than alphabetically.

Sorting numerically or alphabetically

The fastest way to sort a list is to use the Sort Ascending or Sort Descending buttons on the Standard toolbar, as the following steps describe:

1. Move the cell pointer to the column on which you want to base the sort.

2. Click the Sort Ascending button or the Sort Descending button.

Excel sorts the list by the current column.

You may need to sort a list by more than one column. You may, for example, want to sort by month, region, and salesperson. To sort a list on multiple columns, use the procedure that we describe in the preceding steps for each column that you want to sort. Always start with the "least important" column (for example, salesperson) and end with the "most important" column (for example, month).

If you sort a filtered list, Excel sorts only the visible rows. After you remove the filtering from the list, the list is no longer sorted.

If the sorted list contains formulas that refer to cells in other rows in the list, the formulas aren't correct after the sorting. If formulas in your list refer to cells outside the list, make sure that the formulas use an absolute cell reference.

Another way to sort a list is by following these steps:

1. Move the cell pointer anywhere within the list.

2. Choose Data➪Sort.

   Excel displays the Sort dialog box.

3. Select the first sort field from the Sort By drop-down list, and specify Ascending or Descending order by clicking the appropriate radio button.

4. Repeat Step 2 for the second and third sort fields (if you want).

5. Click the Options button, and select any sort options from the Sort Options dialog box that appears, as the following list describes:

   - **First Key Sort Order:** Enables you to specify a custom sort order for the sort.

   - **Case Sensitive:** Makes the sorting case sensitive so that uppercase letters appear before lowercase letters in an ascending sort. Normally, sorting ignores the case of letters.

   - **Orientation:** Enables you to sort by columns rather than by rows (the default).

6. Click OK to return to the Sort dialog box.

7. Click OK, and Excel rearranges the list's rows.

Remember: If the Header row option is set in the Sort dialog box, the sort doesn't affect the first row (field names).

Sorting a list by more than three fields requires an additional step. If you want to sort your list by five fields (Field1, Field2, Field3, Field4, and Field5), start with sorting by Field3, Field4, and Field5. Then re-sort the list by Field1 and Field2. In other words, sort the three "least important" fields first; they remain in sequence as you perform the second sort.

Using a custom sort order

Excel, by default, has four custom lists, and you can define your own. To sort by a custom list, click the Options button in the Sort dialog box; then select the list from the First Key Sort Order drop-down list in the Sort Options dialog box.

Excel custom lists are as follows:

- ✔ **Abbreviated days:** Sun, Mon, Tue, Wed, Thu, Fri, Sat

- ✔ **Days:** Sunday, Monday, Tuesday, Wednesday, Thursday, Friday, Saturday

- ✔ **Abbreviated months:** Jan, Feb, Mar, Apr, May, Jun, Jul, Aug, Sep, Oct, Nov, Dec

- ✔ **Months:** January, February, March, April, May, June, July, August, September, October, November, December

To create a custom list, follow these steps:

1. Choose Tools⇨Options.

2. In the Options dialog box that appears, click the Custom Lists tab.

3. In the Custom Lists list box, select the NEW LIST entry.

4. Enter your list in the List Entries text box.

   Press Enter after you type each entry of the list, or separate each entry with a comma.

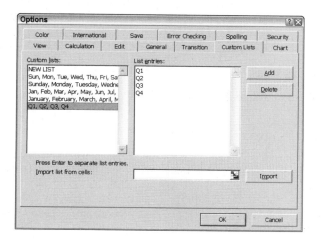

   5. Click Add and then click OK to close the Options dialog box.

After you create your custom list, it becomes available in the First
Key Sort Order drop-down list of the Sort Options dialog box.

If you have a range in your worksheet that you want to save as a
custom sort list, in Step 3, click the Import List from Cells text box,
select the range in the worksheet, and click the Import button.

Goal Seeking and What-If Analysis

What-if analysis refers to the process of changing one or more input cells and observing the effects on formulas. An *input cell* is a cell that a formula uses. If a formula calculates a monthly payment amount for a loan, for example, the formula refers to an input cell that contains the loan amount. *Goal seeking* is the reverse process of what-if analysis. Goal seeking determines the value that an input cell requires to produce a result that you want in a dependent (formula) cell.

In this part . . .

Creating Data Input Tables

Using data tables is an excellent way to perform what-if analyses. Excel's Data Table feature enables you to set up a table to analyze data in the following ways:

- Calculate the results of one *or more* formulas for multiple values of a *single* input

- Calculate the results of a *single* formula for multiple values of *two* inputs

Creating a one-input table

A *one-input data table* displays the results of one or more *result* formulas for multiple values of a single *input cell*. For example, if you have formulas that calculate monthly loan payments, total loan payments, and total loan interest, you can create a data table that shows the results of these formulas for different interest rates. In this case, the interest rate cell is the input cell.

	car loan.xls						
	A	B	C	D	E	F	G
1	Car Loan Calculator						
2							
3	Interest Rate	6.00%			($535.43)	($19,275.34)	($1,675.34)
4	No. of Payments	36		6.00%	($535.43)	($19,275.34)	($1,675.34)
5	Purchase Price	$20,000.00		6.50%	($539.42)	($19,419.21)	($1,819.21)
6	Price + Tax	$21,600.00		7.00%	($543.44)	($19,563.73)	($1,963.73)
7	Down Payment	$4,000.00		7.50%	($547.47)	($19,708.90)	($2,108.90)
8	Net Price	$17,600.00		8.00%	($551.52)	($19,854.72)	($2,254.72)
9				8.50%	($555.59)	($20,001.19)	($2,401.19)
10	Monthly Payment	($535.43)		9.00%	($559.68)	($20,148.31)	($2,548.31)
11	Monthly Payment Formula	=PMT(B3/12,B4,B8)		9.50%	($563.78)	($20,296.08)	($2,696.08)
12				10.00%	($567.90)	($20,444.49)	($2,844.49)
13	Total Payment	($19,275.34)					
14	Total Interest	($1,675.34)					

◄ ► ►│ \ **Loan Sensitivity** / Loan Sensitivity 2 /

The following table describes how the one-input data table is set up:

Table Area	Description
Left column	Values for the single input cell
Top row	Formulas or references to result formulas elsewhere in the worksheet
Upper-left cell	Not used
Remaining cells	Results that Excel enters

Notice that you can interchange the use of the left column and top row — that is, you can enter the values for the single input cell in the top row and enter the formulas or references in the left column.

The simplest way to explain how to set up a one-input data table is by using an example. The previous figure shows how we set up a table by using data from a loan-calculator model. To create the table, follow these steps:

1. In an empty area of your worksheet (or on a separate sheet), enter the values that you want to use for the input cell.

   In the figure, we entered input values in cells D4 through D12.

2. Enter formulas or references to the formulas that you want Excel to calculate for the different input values.

   In the figure, we used formula references. Cell E3 contains the formula =**B10**, cell F3 contains the formula =**B13**, and so on.

3. Select the table range, including the input values in the left column and the formulas in the top row.

4. Choose Data⇨Table from the menu bar.

   Excel displays the Table dialog box.

5. Specify the worksheet cell that you're using as the input value.

   In our example, cell B3 (Interest Rate) is the input cell. Because the values for the input cell are in a column (column D in this case), we used =**B3** in the Column input cell field. We left the Row input cell field blank.

   If the input cell values were in the top row (with the formulas in the left column), you would use the Row input cell field and leave the Column input cell field blank.

6. Click OK.

   Excel performs the calculations and fills in the table.

Remember: Excel uses an array formula that uses the TABLE function. Excel updates the table, therefore, if you change the cell references in the top row or plug in different values in the left column.

See also "Creating a two-input table," immediately following in this part.

Creating a two-input table

A *two-input data table* displays the results of a single formula for various values of two-input cells. If you have a formula that calculates a monthly loan payment, for example, you can create a data table that shows the payment amount for various interest rates and loan amounts. The interest rate cell and the loan amount cell are the input cells.

car loan.xls							
	A	B	C	D	E	F	G
1	Car Loan Calculator						
2							
3	Interest Rate	6.00%		($535.43)	$15,000.00	$18,000.00	$21,000.0
4	No. of Payments	36		6.00%	($456.33)	($547.59)	($638.8
5	Purchase Price	$20,000.00		6.50%	($459.74)	($551.68)	($643.6
6	Price + Tax	$21,600.00		7.00%	($463.16)	($555.79)	($648.4
7	Down Payment	$4,000.00		7.50%	($466.59)	($559.91)	($653.2
8	Net Price	$17,600.00		8.00%	($470.05)	($564.05)	($658.0
9				8.50%	($473.51)	($568.22)	($662.9
10	Monthly Payment	($535.43)		9.00%	($477.00)	($572.40)	($667.7
11	Monthly Payment Formula	=PMT(B3/12,B4,B8)		9.50%	($480.49)	($576.59)	($672.6
12				10.00%	($484.01)	($580.81)	($677.6
13	Total Payment	($19,275.34)					
14	Total Interest	($1,675.34)					

Loan Sensitivity Loan Sensitivity 2

The following table describes how to set up the two-input data table:

Table Area	Description
Left column	Values for the first input cell
Top row	Values for the second input cell
Upper-left cell	Reference to the single result formula
Remaining cells	Results that Excel enters

The simplest way to explain how to set up a two-input data table is by using an example. The previous figure shows how we set up a table by using data from a loan-calculator model. To create the table, follow these steps:

1. **In an empty area of your worksheet (or on a separate sheet), enter the values that you want to use for the first input cell.**

   In the figure, we entered the first input cell values in cells D4 through D12.

2. **Enter the values that you want to use for the second input cell.**

   In the figure, we entered the second input cell values in cells E3 through H3.

3. **In the cell immediately above and to the left of the two input cells (upper-left cell), enter a formula or a reference to the formula that you want Excel to calculate for combinations of the two input values.**

   In the figure, we used a formula reference. Cell D3 contains the formula =**B10**.

4. Select the table range, including the input values in the left column and the input values in the top row.

5. Choose Data⇨Table from the menu bar.

   Excel displays the Table dialog box.

6. Specify the cell for the Row input cell.

   In the figure, the value in the Row input cell is =**B8**.

7. Specify the cell for the Column input cell.

   In the figure, the value in the Column input cell is =**B3**.

8. Click OK.

   Excel performs the calculations and fills in the table.

See also "Creating a one-input table," earlier in this part.

Goal Seeking

Excel's Goal Seek feature enables you to determine the value that a single input cell requires to produce a result that you want in a dependent (formula) cell. If you use the PMT function to calculate the monthly payment of a loan, for example, you may want to determine the loan amount for a specific monthly payment (given a fixed interest rate and payment term). You can adjust the cell that contains the loan amount manually until the formula that contains the PMT function provides the result you want, but using the Goal Seek feature is much faster. The procedure is as follows:

1. Start with a workbook that uses formulas.

2. Choose Tools⇨Goal Seek from the menu bar.

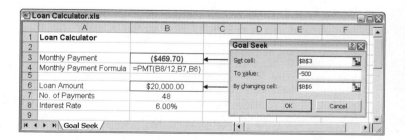

3. Complete the Goal Seek dialog box that appears by specifying the formula cell to change (in the Set Cell text box), the value to change it to (in the To Value text box), and the input cell to change (in the By Changing Cell text box).

4. Click OK.

   Excel displays the solution in the worksheet and in the Goal Seek dialog box.

5. Click OK to replace the original value with the found value; click Cancel to restore your worksheet to the form that it was in before you issued the Tools⇨Goal Seek command.

Remember: Excel can't always find a value that produces the result that you're looking for. (Sometimes a solution doesn't exist.) In such a case, the Goal Seek status box informs you of that fact. If Excel reports that it can't find a solution, but you're pretty sure that one exists, try the following options:

✔ Change the current value of the changing cell to a value that is closer to the solution, and then reissue the command.

✔ Adjust the Maximum iterations setting in the Calculation tab of the Options dialog box (by choosing Tools⇨Options). Increasing the number of iterations makes Excel try other possible solutions.

See also "Creating Data Input Tables," earlier in this part.

Using Scenario Manager

Excel's Scenario Manager feature makes it easy to automate your what-if models. You can store different sets of input values (known as *changing cells*) for any number of variables and give a name to each set. You can then select a set of values by name, and Excel displays the worksheet by using those values. You can generate a summary report that shows the effect of various combinations of values on any number of result cells. The summary report can be an outline or a PivotTable.

Creating a named scenario

To define a scenario, follow these steps:

1. Create your worksheet as usual, using input cells that determine the result of one or more formulas.

2. Choose Tools⇨Scenarios from the menu bar to display the Scenario Manager dialog box.

3. In the Scenario Manager dialog box, click the Add button to add a scenario in the Add Scenario dialog box.

4. Complete the Add Scenario dialog box. The following list describes the settings that are in this dialog box:

- **Scenario Name:** The name for the scenario. You can give it any name that you want.

- **Changing Cells:** The input cells for the scenario. You can enter the cell addresses directly or point to them. Multiple selections are possible, so the input cells don't need to be adjacent to one another. Each named scenario can use the same set of changing cells or different changing cells.

- **Comment:** By default, Excel displays who created the scenario and the date that person created it. You can change this text, add new text to it, or delete it.

- **Protection:** The two Protection options (protecting a scenario and hiding a scenario) are in effect only if the worksheet is protected and the Edit Scenarios check box is deselected in the Protect Sheet dialog box. Protecting a scenario prevents anyone from modifying it; a hidden scenario doesn't appear in the Scenario Manager dialog box. *See also* "Protecting a Worksheet," in Part II.

5. Click OK to display the Scenario Values dialog box.

6. Enter values for the changing cells in the appropriate text boxes.

7. Click the Add button to add the scenario.

8. Repeat Steps 4 through 7 for each additional scenario.

9. Click Close to close the Scenario Manager dialog box.

 An excellent practice is to create names for the changing cells, because names make the cells easier to identify in the Scenario Values dialog box. Names also help make scenario reports more readable.

Remember: The limit to the number of changing cells for a scenario is 32.

See also "Creating a scenario summary report," immediately following in this part.

Creating a scenario summary report

After you define at least two scenarios, you can generate reports that summarize the scenarios by following these steps:

1. Choose Tools⇨Scenarios from the menu bar.

2. Click the Summary button in the Scenario Manager dialog box that appears.

3. Select the type of report, as follows:

    -   **Scenario summary:** The summary report is in the form of an outline.

    -   **Scenario PivotTable:** The summary report is in the form of a PivotTable. This option gives you more flexibility if you define many scenarios with multiple result cells.

4. In the Result Cells text box, specify the summary cells to include in the report and then click OK.

Excel creates a new worksheet to store the summary table.

 An excellent practice is to create names for the result cells, because Excel uses these names in the scenario summary reports that you create. The names help make your reports more readable.

Remember: Result cells must be in the same worksheet as the changing cells.

See also "Creating a named scenario," earlier in this part, and "Creating a PivotTable Report," in Part XIII.

Displaying a named scenario

As you view a scenario, Excel inserts the scenario's values into the changing cells in the worksheet. Formulas that depend on these cells are updated. To view a named scenario, follow these steps:

1. Choose Tools⇨Scenarios from the menu bar.

    Excel displays the Scenario Manager dialog box.

2. Select the scenario from the Scenarios list box, and click Show.

    Excel updates the changing cells in the worksheet by using the scenario's values.

You can view as many scenarios as you want while the Scenario Manager dialog box is open. After you finish, click Close. Values for the last scenario viewed remain in the worksheet.

Analyzing Data with PivotTables

A *PivotTable* report (or simply a *PivotTable*) is a dynamic table that automatically extracts, organizes, and summarizes data from a list. This manipulation enables you to view relationships, make comparisons, detect patterns, and analyze trends among some of or all the fields of data in your list.

In this part . . .

Generally speaking, fields in a database table or list can be one of the following two types:

- ✔ **Data:** Contains a value. A field with the label *TotalSale* or *Amount,* for example, is a data field.

- ✔ **Category:** Describes the data. A field with the label *SalesRep* or *Branch,* for example, is a category field.

See also the introduction to Part XII for an example of a list.

A database table or list can have any number of data fields and any number of category fields. If you create a PivotTable, you usually want to summarize one or more of the data fields. The values in the category fields appear in the PivotTable as rows, columns, or pages.

Adding and Removing Fields in a PivotTable Report

You can add fields to and remove fields from a PivotTable report to change the way it looks or to analyze your data differently.

Inserting a new field

To add a new field to a PivotTable report, follow these steps:

1. Move the cell pointer anywhere within the PivotTable.

2. Drag the new field from the PivotTable Field List to the desired location in the PivotTable.

Removing a field

To remove a field from a PivotTable report, follow these steps:

1. Click the button for the field that you want to remove.

2. Drag the button outside the PivotTable area.

3. Release the mouse button, and Excel updates the PivotTable, removing the field that you dragged away.

Creating a PivotTable Report

Before you can create a PivotTable report from your worksheet, you must set up your worksheet data as a list. **See also** "Working with Lists and External Data," in Part XI, for more information on lists.

To create a PivotTable report from a worksheet list, follow these steps:

1. Move the cell pointer to any cell in the list.

2. Choose Data⇨PivotTable and PivotChart Report.

   Excel displays the first of three dialog boxes.

3. Make sure that the Microsoft Excel List or Database radio button and the PivotTable radio button are both selected, and then click Next.

4. In the second dialog box that appears, make sure that the list range is specified (Excel automatically identifies the database range), and click Next.

5. In the third dialog box, specify the location for the PivotTable report (a new worksheet or an existing worksheet) by clicking the appropriate radio button.

6. Click the Options button to specify additional options (see the first Tip following these steps), and then click Finish.

   Excel displays on-sheet drop zones, a floating PivotTable toolbar, and a PivotTable Field List window that includes the field names from your database.

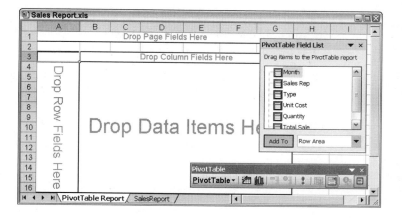

7. Drag the field names that you want to use in your report from the PivotTable Field List window to the appropriate drop zones. Excel outlines the drop zones in blue and labels them for easy identification.

   Excel builds the PivotTable report as you drag the field names to the drop zones.

	A	B	C	D	E
	Sales Report.xls				
1	Sales Rep	(All) ▼			
2					
3	Sum of Total Sale	Type ▼			
4	Month ▼	Existing	New	Grand Total	
5	January	2025	505	2530	
6	February	975	1600	2575	
7	March	1260	1620	2880	
8	April	1820	2380	4200	
9	May	1445	2005	3450	
10	June	3285	4240	7525	
11	Grand Total	10810	12350	23160	
12					

I◄ ◄ ► ►I \ PivotTable Report / SalesR ◄

Depending on the data field that you drag to the data item drop
zone, Excel makes a guess about how you intend to summarize
your data. If you drag a field named TotalSale, for example, Excel
calculates the Sum of TotalSale in the PivotTable. You can override
Excel's choice with a different calculation for the field (count, average max, and so on). To change the data field calculation, double-
click the data field button in the PivotTable (for example, Sum of
TotalSale), select a function in the Summarize by list box of the
PivotTable Field dialog box that appears, and then click OK.

You can dock the PivotTable Field List window by dragging it to the
left or right edge of the worksheet window, and it's then visible only
if the active cell is within the PivotTable report.

Remember: You can drag as many fields as you want to any of the
drop zones, and you don't need to use all the fields. Fields that you
don't use don't appear in the PivotTable report.

Excel includes several options for PivotTable reports, which are
available after you click the Options button in the third step of the
PivotTable Wizard. To access the PivotTable Options dialog box
after you create the PivotTable report, click the PivotTable button
on the PivotTable toolbar and choose Table Options from the drop-
down menu.

You should name the worksheet list if you plan to add more data
later. Then, as you create the PivotTable report, make sure that you
specify the name of the list as you enter the source data range
(Step 2 of the PivotTable and PivotChart Wizard). That way, whenever you add more data to the list, you can update the PivotTable
report to include the new data.

Formatting a PivotTable Report

As you create a PivotTable report, you can choose to apply a default table AutoFormat to the report. (You access the AutoFormat option from the PivotTable Options dialog box that appears after you click the Options button in the third step of the PivotTable Wizard, as we describe in the preceding section.) After Excel creates the PivotTable report, you can specify a different AutoFormat. Excel provides 22 PivotTable AutoFormats.

To change or use an AutoFormat after you create the PivotTable report, select a cell within the PivotTable report and use either of the following methods:

- ✔ Choose Format⇨AutoFormat. This command opens the AutoFormat dialog box with a list of PivotTable AutoFormats. This list replaces the standard worksheet AutoFormats.

- ✔ Click the PivotTable button on the PivotTable toolbar, and choose Format Report from the drop-down menu.

Remember: In creating a PivotTable report, Excel doesn't retain any special number formatting that you may have applied to your original data. If you apply a currency format to your data, for example, and then use that data in the PivotTable, Excel doesn't retain the currency formatting in the PivotTable report.

To change the number format for the data in the PivotTable report, follow these steps:

1. Select any cell in the PivotTable's data area.

2. Right-click and choose Field Settings from the shortcut menu.

   Excel displays its PivotTable Field dialog box.

3. Click the Number button.

   Excel displays the Format Cells dialog box.

4. Select the number format that you need from the Category list box.

5. Click OK to exit the Format Cells dialog box, and click OK to exit the PivotTable Field dialog box.

Remember: Use one of the AutoFormats with the labels Report 1, Report 2, Report 3, and so on to display and/or print a report in indented format, similar to the traditional banded or formatted database report.

Grouping PivotTable Items

A handy feature enables you to group specific items in a single field of a PivotTable report. If one of the fields in your database consists of dates, for example, the PivotTable displays a separate row or column for every date. You may find that grouping the dates into months or quarters and then hiding the details is a more useful way to display them.

To create a group of items in a PivotTable, follow these steps:

1. Select the cells that you want to group.

2. Choose Data⇨Group and Outline⇨Group.

   Excel creates a new field that consists of the selected items. The following figure shows a new field named Quarter 1, which groups January, February, and March.

Sales Report.xls					
	A	B	C	D	E
1	Sales Rep	(All) ▼			
2					
3	Sum of Total Sale		Type ▼		
4	Month 2 ▼	Month ▼	Existing	New	Grand Total
5	Quarter 1	January	2025	505	2530
6		February	975	1600	2575
7		March	1260	1620	2880
8	April	April	1820	2380	4200
9	May	May	1445	2005	3450
10	June	June	3285	4240	7525
11	Grand Total		10810	12350	23160
12					
13					

PivotTable Report / SalesRepo

3. Change the names of the new field and the items by editing them in the Formula Bar if you want.

After you create a group, you can toggle between showing summary data and detail data by double-clicking the group name.

If the items that you want to group aren't next to each other, you can make a multiple selection by pressing and holding Ctrl and then selecting the items that are to make up the group.

If the field items consist of values, dates, or times, you can have Excel do the grouping for you. To create groups automatically, follow these steps:

1. Select any item in the field that you want to group (only one).

2. Choose Data⇨Group and Outline⇨Group.

Excel displays the Grouping dialog box. Excel examines the source data and automatically enters values in the Starting at and Ending at text boxes. The By option is either a text box or a list box, depending on the source data (dates or values).

3. To change the values that Excel suggests, enter the new values in the appropriate text boxes and list box (if applicable).

4. Click OK.

Excel creates the groups.

Remember: If the field items consist of dates or times, all the cells in the date field in the source list must carry a recognized date or time format; otherwise Excel displays an error message if you try to create an automatic group.

Modifying a PivotTable's Structure

A PivotTable report that appears in a worksheet includes the field buttons. You can drag any of the field buttons to a new position in the PivotTable report. (This action is known as *pivoting*). You can, for example, drag a column field to a row position. Excel immediately redisplays the PivotTable report to reflect your change.

You can also change the order of the row fields or the column fields by dragging the buttons. This action affects how the fields nest and can have a dramatic effect on how the table looks.

Remember: A PivotTable is a special type of range, and (except for formatting) you can't make any changes to it. You can't, for example, insert or delete rows, edit results, or move cells. If you attempt to do so, Excel displays an error message.

You can also drag fields from the PivotTable Field List to modify an existing PivotTable's structure.

See also "Creating a PivotTable Report," earlier in this part.

Refreshing a PivotTable Report

If you change the source data that a PivotTable report uses, the PivotTable doesn't update automatically. Instead, you must refresh it manually. To refresh a PivotTable, use any of the following methods:

✓ Choose Data⇨Refresh External Data.

✓ Right-click anywhere in the PivotTable, and choose Refresh External Data from the shortcut menu.

✓ Click the Refresh External Data button on the PivotTable toolbar.

You can have Excel update your PivotTable report automatically every time that you open the worksheet that contains the PivotTable report. Right-click anywhere in the PivotTable report, and choose Table Options from the shortcut menu. Select the Refresh on open check box to activate this option, and click OK.

If you're basing your PivotTable on external data, Excel provides an option to refresh the data automatically every *xxxxx* minutes, where *xxxxx* can be any integer from 1 to 32,767 inclusive. Right-click anywhere in the PivotTable report and choose Table Options from the shortcut menu to access this option.

Glossary: Tech Talk

Absolute reference: In a formula, a row, column or cell reference that doesn't change if you copy the formula to a different cell. An absolute reference uses one or two dollar signs, such as A15 (absolute cell reference), $A15 (absolute column reference) or A$15 (absolute row reference) for cell A15.

Active cell: The cell whose contents appear in the Formula Bar. You can enter information into the active cell and also edit its contents.

Add-in: A file that you load into Excel to provide additional commands or worksheet functions.

Argument: In a worksheet function, information (which you enclose in parentheses) that provides details as to what you want the function to do.

Ask a Question box: A Help tool on the Excel menu bar in which you can type a question in plain English. Excel responds with a list of Help choices.

Auditing: The process of tracking down and correcting errors in your worksheet.

AutoComplete: A tool that enables you to automatically complete a text or mixed text/value entry in a cell based on other entries already made in the same column.

AutoFill: A tool that enables you to fill in several types of data series in a range of cells.

AutoFilter: To display only the rows in a list that meets certain criteria.

AutoFormat: Predefined formatting that you can quickly apply to a range of cells in a worksheet or a pivot table. Also refers to predefined formats that you can apply to a chart.

AutoShape: A graphic object that you place on the draw layer by using one of the Excel drawing tools.

AutoSum tool: A tool that enables you to enter common functions (such as sum, average, count, min and max) quickly.

Cell: A single addressable unit in a worksheet that the intersection of a row and a column defines.

Cell comment: A comment that you attach to a cell.

Cell pointer: The dark border that surrounds the active cell. You move the cell pointer by using the mouse or the arrow keys on the keyboard.

Cell reference: Identifies a cell by giving its column letter and row number. C5, for example, refers to the cell at the intersection of column C and row 5. If you're referring to a cell on a different sheet, you need to precede it with the sheet name and an exclamation point. The cell references can be relative references (most common), absolute references, or mixed references.

Cell tracers: Arrows that show the relationship between the active cell and its related cells (dependents and/or precedents).

Chart: A graphic representation of values in a worksheet. You can embed a chart on a worksheet or store it on a separate chart sheet in a workbook.

Chart element: Parts of a chart with which you can work and modify, such as a data series, axis, gridlines, legend, and so on.

Chart sheet: A type of sheet in a workbook that holds a single chart.

ChartWizard: A series of interactive dialog boxes that help you create charts.

Check box: In a dialog box, an option that you can either turn on or turn off (by clicking it). This item is not the same as a radio (option) button.

Circular reference: In a formula, a reference to the cell that contains the formula (either directly or indirectly). If cell A10 contains =SUM(A1:A10), a circular reference exists because the formula refers to its own cell.

Clipboard: An area of your computer's memory that stores information that you copy or cut from an application. Unlike the Office Clipboard, the standard Windows Clipboard can hold only one piece of data at a time.

Column: Part of a worksheet that consists of 65,536 cells in a vertical arrangement. Each worksheet contains 256 columns.

Conditional formatting: Formatting (such as color or bold text) that you apply to a cell depending on the cell's contents.

Consolidation: The process of merging data from multiple worksheets or multiple workbook files.

Criteria range: A special type of range that holds specifications that an advanced filter uses or that's for a database worksheet function.

Data marker: A bar, area, dot, slice, or other symbol in a chart that represents a single data point or value that originates from a worksheet cell. Related data markers in a chart constitute a data series.

Data series: For a worksheet, refers to the values or text items that Excel fills into a range of cells after you use the AutoFill tool. For a chart, refers to related data points that you plot in the chart.

Data validation: The process of ensuring that the user's entering data of the correct type into a cell. If the entry is outside of a specified range of values, for example, you can display a message to the user.

Database: A systematic collection of information consisting of records (rows) and fields (columns). You can store a database in a worksheet (where it's known as a list) or in an external file.

Default workbook template: A template that you can use as the basis for new workbooks. This template has the name `book.xlt`, and you find it in your `XLStart` folder.

Dependent cell: A cell that contains a formula that refers to the active cell. In other words, the formula depends on the value in the active cell.

Dialog box: An interactive window that appears in response to most commands. Excel uses a dialog box to get additional information from you so that it can carry out the command.

Double-click: To click the left mouse button rapidly twice.

Drag: To press and hold the left mouse button to move an object or extend a selection of cells.

Drag-and-drop: To use the mouse to grab something, move it, and drop it somewhere else. You can use drag-and-drop to move a cell, a range, or a graphic object.

Draw layer: An invisible layer on top of all worksheets. The draw layer contains embedded charts, maps, and drawn objects.

Drop-down list box: In a dialog box, a control that normally shows only one option. If you select this control, a list drops down from it to show more options.

Drop zone (or Drop area): Blue outlined regions (fields) that appear on a worksheet after you finish the steps of the PivotTable and PivotChart Wizard.

Embedded chart: A chart that Excel places on a worksheet's draw layer (instead of it residing on a separate chart sheet).

Error value: A value that begins with a pound sign (#) appearing in a cell, signaling a formula error.

External data range: A range of data that you bring into a worksheet, but that originates outside of Excel, such as in a database, text file or the Web.

External reference: A cell reference to a workbook other than the one in which the reference resides.

Field: In a database, information that Excel contains in columns.

Fill handle: The small, square object that appears at the lower-right corner of the active cell or a selected range of cells.

Filter: To hide rows in a list such that only the rows that meet a certain criteria are visible.

Font: The typeface the Excel uses for text and values.

Footer: A line of information that appears at the bottom of each printed page.

Formatting: The process of changing the appearance of a cell, range, or object.

Formula: An entry in a cell that returns a calculated result.

Formula Bar: The area of Excel, just below the toolbars, that displays the contents of the active cell. You can edit the cell in the Formula Bar.

Function: A special keyword that you use in a formula (SUM, AVEARGE, ROUND and so on) to perform a calculation. Use the Insert Function dialog box to enter a function in a formula.

Functionality: A feature that describes how you publish portions of a worksheet interactively to the Web. Spreadsheet functionality enables you to publish spreadsheet data interactively. PivotTable functionality enables you to publish a pivot table interactively. Chart functionality enables you to publish a Chart interactively. *See also* Interactive Publishing.

Goal seeking: The process of determining the value of a cell that results in a specific value that a formula returns.

Gridlines: Lines that delineate the cells in a worksheet. In a chart, gridlines are extensions of the tick marks on the axes.

Header: A line of information that appears at the top of each printed page.

HTML document: A document that you format for the World Wide Web by using special formatting codes.

Icon: A small picture that you can click with your mouse. (In this book, an icon is a small picture in the left margin that calls your attention to various types of information.)

Import: To retrieve information from a file that was saved by another application.

Interactive Publishing: A feature that publishes data to a Web page in such a way that you can manipulate the data though a browser. By using the Internet Explorer browser, for example, a user can format, sort, or file data in a published spreadsheet or pivot table or make changes to the source data in a published chart that automatically updates the chart.

Legend: In a chart, the small box that describes the data series.

Link formula: A formula that uses a reference to a cell that a different workbook contains.

List: A database that you store in a worksheet. A list contains a header row that describes the contents of the information in each column.

Locked cell: A cell that you can't change if the worksheet is protected. If the worksheet isn't protected, you can modify locked cells.

Margin: The blank space outside the printing area on a page.

Maximize: To make a window as large as it can become.

Menu bar: A special toolbar that contains commands. Normally, the menu bar rests just below the title bar.

Merged cells: Cells that you combine into one larger cell that holds a single value.

Minimize: To make a window as small as it can become.

Mixed reference: In a formula, a reference to a cell that is partially absolute and partially relative. A mixed reference uses one dollar sign, such as A$15 for cell A15. In this case, the column part of the reference is relative; the row part of the reference is absolute.

Mouse pointer: The object that you see move on-screen as you move your mouse. The mouse pointer often changes its shape, depending on what you're doing at the time.

Name Box: A combination text and drop-down list box that resides below the toolbars and to the left of the Formula Bar. You can use this box to define names of cells and ranges or to select a named cell or range.

Named range: A range to which you assign a name. Using named ranges in formulas makes your formulas more readable.

Nested function: A function that uses another function as one of its arguments. In an Excel formula, you can nest a function (so that it contains functions within functions) up to seven levels deep.

Noncontiguous range: A range of cells that don't lie in a single rectangular area. You select a noncontiguous range by pressing Ctrl as you select cells.

Number format: The manner in which a value appears in Excel. You can format a number to appear with a percent sign, for example, and a specific number of decimal places. The number format changes only the appearance of the number (not the number itself).

Office Assistant: A feature in Microsoft Office that provides a variety of interactive Help and assistance with various features.

Office Clipboard: A feature in Microsoft Office that enables you to copy up to 24 items at a time for pasting into any Office application. The last item you copy to the Office Clipboard is also copied to the Windows Clipboard.

Operator: In a formula, a character that represents the type of operation that you intend to perform. Operators include + (plus sign), / (division sign), & (text concatenation), and others.

Operator precedence: The order in which Excel performs operations in formulas.

Option button: *See* Radio button.

Outline: A worksheet that you structure in such a way that you can expand information (to show additional details) or contract it (to show fewer details).

Page break: A dashed line that appears on-screen to tell you where the pages break as you print the worksheet. Page breaks are either natural or those that you can specify manually.

Page Break Preview mode: An editable view that superimposes page numbers and page breaks on the worksheet. You can drag the page breaks to move them.

Pane: One part of a worksheet window that's split into either two or four parts.

Paste: To retrieve information that you copied or cut and stored on the Clipboard.

PivotTable report: A table that summarizes information that a worksheet list or external database contains.

Pointing: The process of selecting a range by using either the keyboard or the mouse. If you need to enter a cell or range reference into a dialog box, you can either enter it directly or point to it in the worksheet.

Precedent cell: A cell that a formula cell refers to. A single formula can have many precedent cells, and the precedents can be direct or indirect.

Print Area: One or more ranges of cells that you designate to print if you don't want to print the entire worksheet.

Print titles: One or more rows and/or columns that appear on each page of printed output.

Protected workbook: A workbook that prevents users from making changes to workbook elements and optionally prevents users from viewing and editing the workbook.

Protected worksheet: A worksheet in which you restrict elements, such as cells with formulas, from user access.

Radio button: In a dialog box, one of a group of buttons. You can select only one button in the group at any time. Also known as *option buttons*.

Range: A collection of two or more cells. Specify a range by separating the upper-left cell and the lower-right cell with a colon.

Range Finder: The colored frame that indicates cells that a formula references or that a chart uses. You can grab and move the frame to change the formula or chart series.

Recalculate: To update a worksheet's formulas by using the most current values.

Record: In a database, information that lies in rows.

Redo: To reverse the effects of an Undo operation.

Refreshable data: Worksheet data that you can update from an external data source.

Relative reference: In a formula, a reference to a cell that changes (in a relative manner) if you copy the formula to a different cell. A relative reference doesn't use any dollar signs (as does an absolute reference or a mixed reference).

Restore: To return a window (either the Excel window or a workbook window) to its previous size.

Right-click: To click the right mouse button.

Row: Part of a worksheet that consists of 256 cells in a horizontal arrangement. Each worksheet contains 65,536 rows.

Scenario: A specific set of values for input cells. You assign each scenario a name and can display it by using the Excel scenario manager.

ScreenTip: Text that pops-up on-screen to provide information on selected elements (toolbar buttons, dialog box options, and so on).

Scroll bar: One of two bars (on the right and bottom of a workbook window) that enable you to scroll quickly through the worksheet by using the mouse.

Selection: The item that's currently active. A selection can consist of a cell or range, a part of a chart, or one or more graphic objects.

Shared workbook: A workbook set up to enable multiple users on a network to view and make changes at the same time.

Sheet: One unit of a workbook, which can consist of a worksheet or a chart sheet. Activate a sheet by clicking its sheet tab.

Shortcut menu: The context-sensitive menu that appears after you right-click a cell, range, or object.

Smart Tag: A button that appears when the user needs it (such as when a user makes an error in a formula or pastes some data) and gives the user the options they need to change the given action or error.

Sort: To rearrange the order of rows, basing the arrangement on the contents of one or more columns. You can conduct sorts in ascending or descending order.

Spreadsheet: A generic term for a product such as Excel that you use to track and calculate data. People often use this term to refer to a worksheet or a workbook.

Status bar: The line at the bottom of the Excel window that shows the status of several things and also displays some messages.

Style: A combination of formatting characteristics, such as font, font size, and indentation, that you name and store as a set. If you apply a style, Excel applies all the formatting instructions in that style at one time.

Task pane: A window that enables you perform certain tasks quickly and easily, such as opening new workbooks, searching for text in files and pasting items that you first copy to the Office Clipboard.

Template: A file that you use as the basis for a new workbook. Examples include the Spreadsheet Solutions templates that come with Excel.

Text attributes: Formats that you apply to cell contents. These attributes include bold, underline, italic, and strikethrough.

Text file: A file that contains data only and no formatting. A text file is sometimes known as an ASCII file.

Title bar: The colored bar at the top of every window. Drag the title bar by using the mouse to move a nonmaximized window.

Toolbar: A collection of buttons that serve as shortcuts for common commands.

Trendline: A graphic representation of trends in data series, such as a line sloping upward to represent increased sales over a period of months. You use trendlines for the study of problems of prediction, also known as regression analysis.

Undo: To reverse the effects of the last command (or as many as 16 of the previous commands) by using the Edit➪Undo menu command (or pressing Ctrl+Z).

Value: A number that you enter into a cell.

Watch Window: A window that enables you to view cells and their formulas, especially if the cells are out of view.

Web query: A query that retrieves data that resides on your intranet, the Internet, or the World Wide Web.

What-if analysis: The process of changing one or more input cells and observing the effects on one or more dependent formulas. The Excel Scenario Manager and Data Input table features enable you to easily to perform what-if analyses.

Window: A container for an application or a workbook. You can move and resize windows.

Windows Clipboard: *See* Clipboard.

Wizard: A series of dialog boxes that assist you in performing an operation such as creating a chart, importing text, or creating certain types of formulas.

Workbook: The name for a file that Excel uses. A workbook consists of one or more sheets.

Worksheet: A sheet in a workbook that contains cells. Worksheets are the type of sheets that you use most commonly.

Workspace file: A file that contains information about all open workbooks: their size, arrangement, and position. You can save a workspace file and then re-open it to pick up where you left off.

Zoom: To expand or contract the size of the text appearing in a window. Zoom in to make text larger, and zoom out to make text smaller so that you can see more.

Index

FOR DUMMIES®

PERSONAL FINANCE & BUSINESS

Investing
0-7645-2431-3

Home Buying
0-7645-5331-3

Grant Writing
0-7645-5307-0

Also available:

Accounting For Dummies
(0-7645-5314-3)

Business Plans Kit For
Dummies
(0-7645-5365-8)

Managing For Dummies
(1-5688-4858-7)

Mutual Funds For
Dummies
(0-7645-5329-1)

QuickBooks All-in-One
Desk Reference For
Dummies
(0-7645-1963-8)

Resumes For Dummies
(0-7645-5471-9)

Small Business Kit For
Dummies
(0-7645-5093-4)

Starting an eBay Business
For Dummies
(0-7645-1547-0)

Taxes For Dummies 2003
(0-7645-5475-1)

HOME, GARDEN, FOOD & WINE

Feng Shui
0-7645-5295-3

Gardening
0-7645-5130-2

Cooking
0-7645-5250-3

Also available:

Bartending For Dummies
(0-7645-5051-9)

Christmas Cooking For
Dummies
(0-7645-5407-7)

Cookies For Dummies
(0-7645-5390-9)

Diabetes Cookbook For
Dummies
(0-7645-5230-9)

Grilling For Dummies
(0-7645-5076-4)

Home Maintenance For
Dummies
(0-7645-5215-5)

Slow Cookers For
Dummies
(0-7645-5240-6)

Wine For Dummies
(0-7645-5114-0)

FITNESS, SPORTS, HOBBIES & PETS

Fitness
0-7645-5167-1

Golf
0-7645-5146-9

Guitar
0-7645-5106-X

Also available:

Cats For Dummies
(0-7645-5275-9)

Chess For Dummies
(0-7645-5003-9)

Dog Training For
Dummies
(0-7645-5286-4)

Labrador Retrievers For
Dummies
(0-7645-5281-3)

Martial Arts For Dummies
(0-7645-5358-5)

Piano For Dummies
(0-7645-5105-1)

Pilates For Dummies
(0-7645-5397-6)

Power Yoga For Dummies
(0-7645-5342-9)

Puppies For Dummies
(0-7645-5255-4)

Quilting For Dummies
(0-7645-5118-3)

Rock Guitar For Dummies
(0-7645-5356-9)

Weight Training For
Dummies
(0-7645-5168-X)

Available wherever books are sold.
Go to www.dummies.com or call 1-877-762-2974 to order direct

WILEY

FOR DUMMIES®

A world of resources to help you grow

TRAVEL

Italy
FOR DUMMIES
0-7645-5453-0

Hawaii
FOR DUMMIES
0-7645-5438-7

Walt Disney World & Orlando
FOR DUMMIES
0-7645-5444-1

Also available:

America's National Parks
For Dummies
(0-7645-6204-5)

Caribbean For Dummies
(0-7645-5445-X)

Cruise Vacations For
Dummies 2003
(0-7645-5459-X)

Europe For Dummies
(0-7645-5456-5)

Ireland For Dummies
(0-7645-6199-5)

France For Dummies
(0-7645-6292-4)

Las Vegas For Dummies
(0-7645-5448-4)

London For Dummies
(0-7645-5416-6)

Mexico's Beach Resorts
For Dummies
(0-7645-6262-2)

Paris For Dummies
(0-7645-5494-8)

RV Vacations For
Dummies
(0-7645-5443-3)

EDUCATION & TEST PREPARATION

Spanish
FOR DUMMIES
0-7645-5194-9

Algebra
FOR DUMMIES
0-7645-5325-9

U.S. History
FOR DUMMIES
0-7645-5249-X

Also available:

The ACT For Dummies
(0-7645-5210-4)

Chemistry For Dummies
(0-7645-5430-1)

English Grammar For
Dummies
(0-7645-5322-4)

French For Dummies
(0-7645-5193-0)

GMAT For Dummies
(0-7645-5251-1)

Inglés Para Dummies
(0-7645-5427-1)

Italian For Dummies
(0-7645-5196-5)

Research Papers For
Dummies
(0-7645-5426-3)

SAT I For Dummies
(0-7645-5472-7)

U.S. History For Dummies
(0-7645-5249-X)

World History For
Dummies
(0-7645-5242-2)

HEALTH, SELF-HELP & SPIRITUALITY

Diabetes
FOR DUMMIES
0-7645-5154-X

Sex
FOR DUMMIES
0-7645-5302-X

Parenting
FOR DUMMIES
0-7645-5418-2

Also available:

The Bible For Dummies
(0-7645-5296-1)

Controlling Cholesterol
For Dummies
(0-7645-5440-9)

Dating For Dummies
(0-7645-5072-1)

Dieting For Dummies
(0-7645-5126-4)

High Blood Pressure For
Dummies
(0-7645-5424-7)

Judaism For Dummies
(0-7645-5299-6)

Menopause For Dummies
(0-7645-5458-1)

Nutrition For Dummies
(0-7645-5180-9)

Potty Training For
Dummies
(0-7645-5417-4)

Pregnancy For Dummies
(0-7645-5074-8)

Rekindling Romance For
Dummies
(0-7645-5303-8)

Religion For Dummies
(0-7645-5264-3)